Pillars of Wealth

Personal Finance Essentials for Medical Professionals

Revised Edition

Yuval Bar-Or, PhD

TLB Publishing

Copyright 2017 by Yuval Bar-Or

Cover photo: Barbara Glaeser

Cover by: Creative Jestures

Library of Congress Control Number: 2013923519

Library of Congress Cataloging-in-Publication Data

Bar-Or, Yuval, 1967-

Pillars of Wealth: Personal Finance Essentials for Medical Professionals / Yuval Bar-Or

p.   cm.

ISBN: 978-0-9800118-9-0

1. Personal finance 2. Wealth management 3. Estate planning 4. Financial literacy 5. Risk management
    I. Title.

Books are available at wholesale discounts to educational institutions, corporations, and non-profits. For information, please contact us at: yuval@pillarsofwealth.com.

In memory of my father
Oded Bar-Or, MD
1937 - 2005

Acknowledgements

The *Pillars of Wealth* book series was made possible through the willingness of many busy professionals to share their experiences and advice. I thank Cynthia Mullen, MD, Ken Lewis, Charles Feitel, Jeanne Sanders, Nathan Crowe, Wayne Zell, Brett Weiss, Jeffrey Hausfeld, MD, Martin Wasserman, MD, Gareth Petsch, Don McDaniel, David Kovel, Dan D'Orazio, Christopher DeMarco, Ph.D., Andrew Giddens, Allen Schiff, Michael Limsky, Barry Rosen, Abba Poliakoff, Aaron Horne, MD, Sammy Zakaria, MD, Rani Hasan, MD, Ben Bashiri, Kirk Siegwarth, Thomas Sessa, Gai Cole, Rajiv Mahajan, Samuel Luxenburg, Michaela Muffoletto, David Leichter, Jeffrey Ring, Sanford Fisher, Robert Giuntoli, MD, Michael Simmons, Taylor Shoffner, Melissa Elliott, DDS, Xian Zoey Gao, Qi Li, Mark Rapson, and Manuel Peregrino, MD.

Special thanks to Dipan Desai, MD, for his assistance with the book manuscript—in particular the health care industry chapter—and for his shared vision of delivering the subject matter to dozens of physicians at Johns Hopkins University's School of Medicine.

Life is short, art long, opportunity fleeting,
experience treacherous, judgment difficult.

— Hippocrates

Table of Contents

Introduction 1

What Is This Book About? 1

Why Did I Write This Book Series? 3

Who Is This Book For? 4

The Axioms & Time Value of Money 5

Axiom 1: Your Most Valuable Asset is Earning Capacity 5

Axiom 2: Your Most Precious Resource is Time 6

Axiom 3: Your Greatest Enemy is Procrastination 8

Pillars of Wealth 13

The Pillars of Wealth Objective 17

Stocks and Bonds Pillar 19

Cash Pillar 20

Real Estate Pillar 24

Direct Business Ownership Pillar 26

College Savings Pillar 27

Insurance Cash Value Pillar 29

Annuities Pillar 30

Collectibles Pillar 33

Anticipated Inheritance Pillar 34

Precarious Pillars 35

Diversified Pillars 38

Where Do The Pillars Come From? 38

Credential Management 39

Pillar of Strength – Your Spouse or Partner 41

Investing Basics & Account Types 43

Investment Strategies 44

Investment Account Types 45

Some Thoughts on American Stock Market Returns 49

Professional Development Timeline 53

Medical/Dental Student 53

Intern/Resident/Fellow 54

First 'Real' Job 56

Managerial/Ownership Role 60

Managing Debt – Don't Let Your Pillars Sink 63

Repaying Student Loans 65

Car Purchase vs. Lease 70

Mortgage Debt 71

Credit Cards 75

Your Credit Score 76

Managing Risk – Anticipating Threats to Your Pillars 79

What is Risk? 80

What is Return? 81

Risk Tolerance, Risk Aversion, Risk Appetite 82

Measuring Return 85

Measuring Risk 88

Financial Advisors Rarely Understand Risk's Nuances 91

Is Risk Good or Bad?..92

Risk Handling Alternatives..94

Financial Decision Making..97

Decision Making Paradigms..98

Psychological Barriers to Decision Making 99

First Lines of Defense...106

Final Thoughts on Decision Making 108

Reviewing Your Employment Contract 109

Compensation 109

Benefits..112

Medical Malpractice Insurance 114

Termination Circumstances 116

Non-Compete & Non-Solicitation...116

Integration & Fraud..117

Indemnification...117

Business Ownership..117

Final Thoughts on Employment Contracts..........................118

Estate Planning – Transferring Pillars to Others 121

Basic Estate Planning Documents 122

Tax Planning...126

Asset Protection Planning...128

Final Thoughts on Asset Protection......................................131

The American Health Care Industry...133

History of Health Insurance in the U.S................................133

Structure of the American Health Care Industry.................134

Medicare...135

Medicaid..136

Physician Compensation...136

The Patient Protection and Affordable Care Act 138

Insurance – Protecting Your Pillars 143

    What Exactly is Insurance For? 144

    Identifying Good Insurance Companies 145

    Insurance Types 146

    Key Features & Terminology 147

    Disability Insurance 150

    Property and Casualty Insurance 153

    Life Insurance 154

    Long-Term Care Insurance 166

    Final Thoughts on Insurance 168

Working With a Financial Advisor 169

    DIY versus Using an Advisor 170

    The Basic Functions of Financial Advisors 171

    The Fundamental Characteristics of Advisors 173

    Reclassifying Advisors 179

    Finding Advisors 180

    Your Responsibilities 186

    If You Seek Advice – Find an Expert 187

Work-Life Balance 189

    Take Your Own Advice 190

    Participate in Home Life 190

    Words of Wisdom 191

Building Pillars Requires Advance Planning 195

Appendix 1: Personal (Household) Budgets 199

    Budget Instructions 199

    Medical Student Budget 200

    Intern/Resident/Fellow Budget 202

    First 'Real' Job Budget 203

Manager/Owner Budget.. 205

Appendix 2: Basic Economics Concepts........................ 207

References and Online Resources 223

Introduction

What Is This Book About?

Most doctors complete their residency or fellowship without sufficient knowledge of business and finance. This educational deficiency often leads them to make sub-optimal decisions, and leaves them vulnerable to unqualified or unscrupulous salespeople pitching a variety of financial products.

The objective of this book is to equip you with the basic knowledge needed to make better financial decisions for yourself and your family.

There are many books on the subject of financial literacy. Unfortunately, the vast majority of them are written by finance professionals—people who want to sell you insurance or investment management services. Because of this sales agenda, you can't trust those books to provide balanced discussions of important topics. Industry professionals also often offer free so-called 'education' sessions. In reality, their events are thinly veiled marketing efforts.

In contrast, I am an educator. In creating the *Pillars of Wealth* content, my focus is exclusively on objective, scientifically sound education. I don't sell financial products. As you will see, *Pillars of Wealth* is not a gimmick—it's a metaphor; one that has proven useful during my many years of teaching finance to various audiences.

A major challenge for those seeking and teaching financial literacy is that the financial information we encounter in the public domain is often reduced to sound bites or snippets by the media, sales people, and politicians. Generalizations and pithy one-liners lead to a false sense of order and certainty. In reality, there is far more chaos, complexity and nuance in the world of finance. For example, rising interest rates don't always lead to higher unemployment rates, purchasing life insurance isn't always good or always bad for all households, and investing in real estate is neither always a good idea nor always a bad idea.

This book aims to provide a balanced discussion that recognizes subtleties and doesn't resort to reflexive emotional responses. Ultimately, this book is about helping you to level the playing field. You don't need to become a financial expert. You don't need to compromise your science or patient focus. All you need to know are the basics. These will help you determine whether you *can* and *should* make decisions on your own, which questions to ask, and how to evaluate prospective providers of financial services in the event you elect to use their services.

There are significant and direct benefits to taking control of your financial planning. Better decisions can mean smoother interactions with financial services providers, a happier home, earlier retirement, and greater financial freedom.

The benefits of good decision making are incremental and compound over long time horizons. It follows that making poor decisions (and even just slightly suboptimal ones) and allowing them to fester, severely undermines your financial health. It's far more effective to make better decisions early on than having to make up for lost time later.

As a doctor your typical priorities are likely to be:

1. Provide high quality care to patients
2. Get desired medical outcomes
3. Keep patient waiting-times low
4. Keep up with literature, pursue continuing education
5. Avoid lawsuits
6. Spend time with family …
100. Learn about business, finance, and economics

The reality, of course, is that life throws financial challenges at us without warning, forcing us to quickly switch priorities. The absence of basic knowledge, combined with time pressure, is likely to result in suboptimal and sometimes even devastating financial decisions.

As a doctor, you understand more than most that practicing preventative (proactive) medicine is far better than reactive medicine. If you wish to deal more proactively with household financial matters, then this book is for you. If you wish to improve the financial wellbeing of your private practice, please refer to the second book in this series: *Pillars of Wealth Book II: Finance and Business Essentials for Medical Practices.*

Additional information, including access to online education, may be found at www.PillarsOfWealth.com.

Why Did I Write This Book Series?

My father was a renowned physician, widely recognized as the world's leader in his field of pediatric exercise physiology. With close to 200 peer-reviewed publications, he was a prolific researcher and popular lecturer who lived and breathed academic medicine. He was an old-fashioned doctor, who cared deeply about doing good, and was universally respected and loved by his family, students, staff and patients. He was also a very trusting and honest person, which made him an ideal target for brokers, agents, and advisors pitching a plethora of financial products and services.

After his untimely passing at the age of 67, I watched my mother struggle. Observing her struggles (and recognizing that she was in relatively good shape compared to most widows) made me realize just how vulnerable physician families are. This led to a career change, as I gradually extricated myself from the world of financial risk management (effectively, I was a 'physician' for corporations) and rededicated myself to improving financial literacy among medical professionals.

I began by delivering workshops, participating in blogs, functioning as a consumer advocate, and making media appearances. I even obtained the same licenses required of financial advisors so I could truly understand the business of retail financial services and the people providing those services (I have since allowed those licenses to expire). My personal voyage culminated in the *Pillars of Wealth* initiative, whose objective is to help you and your family attain the prosperity you desire.

Many doctors neglect financial decision making due to lack of time, lack of interest, and in some cases, a general sense of intimidation. In response, many seek to outsource all financial decision making to a reliable financial advisor. In a perfect world this would be an ideal solution. In the real world some financial advisors are inept, some are conflicted, and some are downright dishonest.

Are you able to distinguish the good from the bad? Are you sure your best friend, in-law, or work colleague can help you do this reliably? The honest answers in most cases are 'no.'

The safest solution for you is to gain more knowledge. That knowledge empowers you and reduces your reliance on those who may not have your best interests at heart.

Prior to publication, the working title of this book was 'Sitting Ducks.' This reflected the feeling among many medical professionals that they are viewed by financial service providers as high potential targets who need services desperately (yet don't have the time or inclination to fully understand them). To a great extent, these books are my response to the anxiety and helplessness felt by friends and family members. My hope is that the content of this book series will help you understand relevant issues and take appropriate actions to protect your family.

Who Is This Book For?

This book is directed at all health care professionals, including physicians, dentists, pharmacists, and veterinarians. For brevity I will use *doctor* to refer to all readers.

More broadly, the information in this book is appropriate for any professional who shares certain characteristics with medical practitioners, including: Spending a lot of time in school, and therefore beginning earnings later than other professions, carrying a lot of school debt, working long hours in potentially absorbing and stressful environments, and having the potential for high lifetime earnings and therefore a need to utilize asset protection and tax management techniques.

Other professionals who may share these characteristics include: attorneys, engineers, and information technology specialists, among others.

The Axioms & Time Value of Money

There are three axioms which you must keep in mind at all times in order to make better financial decisions:

Axiom 1: Your Most Valuable Asset is Earning Capacity

When asked to name their most important financial asset, many people say 'my home' (or 'my car').

Yes, a home can be a significant financial asset, but the value of a home pales in comparison to your lifetime *earning capacity* or *earning potential*. A doctor who earns $300,000 per year over 30 years has a lifetime earning capacity of $9 million. Compare this to a home with a value of $400,000 and you can clearly see that the human financial asset is by far more important.

Protect Your Lifetime Earnings

All professionals invest in themselves. Economists refer to this as developing *human capital*. One of the distinguishing features of doctors is that they spend more time and money and effort on building their human capital than most other professions. Your return on this investment comes in the form of lifetime earnings you receive. Those lifetime earnings are needed to: pay off student debt, cover a home mortgage, make car payments, fund children's college education, and provide enough for a comfortable retirement. It is therefore crucial to safeguard that earnings capacity. The insurance section covers these issues in greater detail.

Axiom 2: Your Most Precious Resource is Time

Medical students commit to a very lengthy and demanding educational process. They learn very quickly that there just aren't enough hours in a day. Not only do they face very rigorous academic challenges, they are also painfully aware that if they don't force themselves to make time for social activities and exercise, they may blink and find themselves twelve years older and without a life.

As students and doctors strive to balance hectic lives, they have little time for anything else. And that, of course, is why on the eve of completing residencies and fellowships, many doctors find themselves unprepared to make important financial decisions including how to prioritize repayment of student loans, whether and how to afford a new home and or car, how to take the first steps toward launching a private practice, etc.

The last thing doctors want to do is spend precious time on activities they find boring or frustrating. But making some time for critical decisions can make life easier down the road, and most importantly—can save time in the long-term, by obviating the need to make hurried or panicked decisions, or spending time fixing mistakes.

The best way to save time is to be organized, responsible, grounded in reality, and open to objective knowledge that will make you a more efficient decision maker.

Be Organized

At the very least, you should have one drawer where you throw all financial agreements, contracts, receipts, etc. Always get a receipt! It's easy to stuff it in your pocket and transfer it to the drawer or file when you empty your pockets at the end of the day. Even better (and really the recommended solution) is to have a file or folder for each financial account or product. For example, keep a file for each property and casualty insurance product (homeowner's or renter's insurance, auto insurance, and umbrella insurance). Similarly, maintain folders for life insurance, disability insurance, your home mortgage, college saving plan, and one for each brokerage, investment, IRA, 401(k), or 403(b) account. You don't even need to actively do anything with these folders: you don't need to examine them on a daily basis—just make sure you put all relevant correspondence including the latest statements in each folder.

You should also have a file for each tax year, into which you should put all receipts and any other obviously tax-relevant information such as W2 and 1099 documents sent by employers. This doesn't require any mental energy on your part, it is simply filing. But this discipline will make it much easier to take action whenever you are ready to do so in future. You can bring these files to your financial advisor and/or accountant, and let them sort through and determine what's relevant. As your knowledge grows you can gradually take greater ownership of these documents and pore over them yourself.

Getting into the habit of good organization will serve you well in future. One specific example is that if you are ever audited by the IRS, the receipts and records you keep are your first line of defense and they will save you and your accountant time, headaches, and money.

Be Responsible

There are countless stories of dentists and physicians living beyond their means. One case that immediately comes to mind is that of two plastic surgeon partners. Both were consistently earning $800,000 annually, yet had less than $700 in the bank. Inconceivably (at least for most of us), they'd spent all their money on gargantuan real estate and expensive automobiles (one of them owned seven cars).

While real estate can be an investment, keep in mind that the cost of a home doesn't end with the purchase. If there's a mortgage, you are obligating yourself to making a long stream of principal and interest payments over 15 to 30 years. You are also responsible for property taxes each year (trophy homes have very high taxes). And, you must also constantly pay for utilities and maintenance of each property.

Take the advice many professional athletes are given: you are allowed one of everything, one home, one car, one loud piece of jewelry, one spouse, and … you get the picture.

Consider the two plastic surgeons described above. Had they lived modestly, and meticulously saved their significant earnings, each of them could have realistically saved four to five million dollars over ten years. They could have retired, very comfortably, at the age of 45! Instead, they became slaves to house and car payments by over-extending themselves.

One of the first purchases some doctors make (upon taking their first well-compensated job after residency) is to buy a nice car. There is no doubt that you deserve to enjoy the fruits of your long and difficult labors, but an expensive car is generally not the most responsible move when carrying $150,000 of school debt. We'll revisit this issue later.

Be Grounded In Reality and Seek Objective Knowledge

There's a saying on Wall Street that "money doesn't grow on trees." The point is that if an investment opportunity sounds too good to be true—it probably is too good to be true. Greed makes us want to believe otherwise. But chasing such 'opportunities' is almost always a waste of time (and our hard-earned) money. The best protection against self-destructive tendencies is to remain grounded and to surround ourselves with objective facts. Facts make it easier to resist the seductive appeal of what appears to be 'easy money.'

Doctors understand the importance of knowledge because arguably more than any other profession, in medicine knowledge is the power over life and death. Knowledge doesn't just allow you to understand financial products. It's also crucial for protecting yourself against insincere agents, brokers, and advisors.

Axiom 3: Your Greatest Enemy is Procrastination

In the same way that ignoring a disease and allowing it to fester is bad medicine, ignoring and delaying financial decisions is bad household management.

Yes, doctors are smarter than average, and they have higher than average earning capacity. But, like all other people, doctors *can* get sick or disabled, they *can* contract a terminal illness or die prematurely due to a tragic accident. They can also find themselves close to age 65 without a nest egg sufficient for a dignified retirement.

Some real examples: I recall as a child, when one of my father's best friends, a physician in his 40s, diagnosed his own terminal illness. He did not have life insurance. Another family friend, a surgeon, developed a tremor and could no longer operate. He did not have appropriate disability insurance.

The only response to these statistical inevitabilities is to be prepared, which is to say—not to procrastinate.

Why Doctors Procrastinate?

Doctors are always busy. It's easy to be distracted by: saving people's lives, attending to the well being of your own family, trying to find time to exercise, manage a medical practice, teach medical students, prepare and deliver lectures, write articles, etc.

When doctors do finally have a spare moment, they are often fatigued and unable to focus on financial decisions. After an intense and long day they come home to a crying baby and tired spouse (or tired baby and crying spouse)—not a setting that lends itself to reading and learning about financial decision making.

Let's face it. Finance is not a stimulating subject for most people. Most people find financial decisions confusing and frustrating, leading to a natural reaction—putting them off.

Perhaps most importantly, doctors are actually trained to put off taking action. (Yes, really!) Consider the "first, do no harm" tenet of medical science. This is a procrastination principle (Yes, I know there is a very profound element to this guideline, which I am ignoring, but please bear with me). Doctors are trained not to interfere when the body's natural defenses appear to be doing their job, or there is a chance they can do their job. So as long as a patient appears to be stable, not taking any action (what I'm calling procrastination) can be the best strategy. Rather than engaging in intrusive surgery or administration of powerful drugs with potentially harmful side effects, the order of the day is—do nothing—let the body heal itself if possible.

But outside the field of medicine, and in particular in the business and investing world, procrastination is the insidious unseen killer. It steadily undermines our financial health, and its effects are often only realized years later when it's no longer possible to make up for lost time. To understand this fully, we need to examine the time value of money.

Understand the Time Value of Money

Time Value of Money is arguably the most important concept for a consumer of financial services. It begins with the observation that a particular sum of money has different value or purchasing power depending on when it is received. A dollar received today is worth more than a dollar received a year from now, because I can take today's dollar and invest it and at year's end I will have my dollar plus whatever interest I've earned.

While this very basic concept appears trivial, it's far more momentous than most people realize. Let's assume a dollar is invested at 6% interest annually, and that all earned interest is reinvested over the course of many years at the same rate of return. After 12 years that single dollar doubles to two dollars. After another 12 years the value doubles again. This dramatic (100%) increase in value every 12 years is due primarily to compounding of interest over an extended period of time. Keep in mind that your only investment in this example was one dollar. After 24 years you have realized a 300% return (1 dollar became 4). If the interest rate is just over 7% annually, the investment value doubles every ten years instead of twelve.

Let's apply this to your home. You buy a home for $200,000 today and it appreciates in value at 7% annually. Twenty years from now that home would be worth around $800,000.

Similarly, any stock and bond investments you make can be *expected* to appreciate in value over time. ('Expected' is not the same as 'guaranteed'). When you invest steadily each year, you are planting a new seed of growth with each cash injection. Each of those seeds grows and compounds. The longer you invest, the more dramatic the potential effect of compounding. This observation underlies the importance of beginning to save and invest as early as possible, because those early dollars have the most time to grow.

Figure 1 shows the value of $1,000 dollars invested at 6% (solid line) and 8% (dashed line) annual returns. $1,000 invested at 6% grows over 30 years to just under $6,000. At an 8% growth rate, that single $1,000 initial investment grows to around $10,000.

Note the steeper growth in later years (evident especially in the 8% growth case). This is where the benefits of compounding are strongest. While the lower interest rate (6%) leads to a lower total accumulation in later years, there is still significant compounding growth.

Figure 1: $1,000 Compounded at 6% and 8%

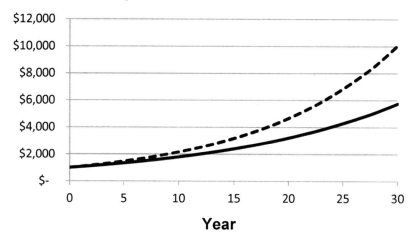

If you invested $1,000 *every* year for 30 years, each would compound for the remainder of the timeline. That is, your first $1,000 would compound over 30 years, the second over 29 years, and so on. Assuming consistent 8% growth throughout, the aggregate *total* nest egg generated this way over 30 years would be just over $120,000.

Suppose you intended this to be your plan but that first year you decided to buy a fancy coffee maker instead of investing $1,000. The loss to your future nest egg would not be $1,000. Rather, the decrease in your future nest egg would be the $10,000 that initial investment would have grown to. This emphasizes the point that dollars you set aside early are the most powerful in terms of growth potential. From a cumulative future next egg perspective, you'd actually be better off making that initial $1,000 investment and instead skipping the last seven $1,000 installments! The conclusion is that even if you can only put aside small amounts in the early years, these small amounts have the potential to become large building blocks in your retirement nest egg in the future.

We've just seen how powerfully time value of money can work in your favor when you *invest*. But it can work against you when you *borrow* money. The obvious example is borrowing to finance your education.

Many residents and fellows elect to defer payments on their undergraduate and medical school loans. While they don't pay interest during the deferral period, that interest is instead being added to their total debt (known as *capitalization*). This means that down the road, they will be paying interest *on* that accrued interest. The more the mountain of debt grows, the higher their monthly payments will be and the longer it will take to pay off those loans.

Be Proactive

In my experience, those doctors who found themselves in better shape a decade into work life are those who were proactive and made decisions promptly. Procrastination leads to many negative outcomes, none of which may seem obvious at the time, but all of which are insidiously conspiring to undermine your nest egg.

In both medicine and finance, it's more effective and less costly to anticipate and be prepared rather than be surprised and have to react. It's much better to get a skateboarding child a pair of wrist guards than have to treat that child's broken wrist. Similarly, it's much better to understand financial risks and proactively take steps to avoid or mitigate them than to play catch up after a deep loss is realized.

Pillars of Wealth

The *Pillars of Wealth* concept helps to frame the overall financial planning discussion. Pillars of wealth are the various financial assets we accumulate over our lifetime. These assets are akin to pillars that hold up or support our retirement. They are also repositories for any wealth we wish to pass to our heirs or to charitable organizations.

It follows that our overall objective should be to collect as many different pillars as possible.

Our pillars of wealth (or assets) may be tracked using a *balance sheet*. A typical personal balance sheet consists of two columns. The left column lists personal assets, which may include a home, a car, some stock and bond investments, etc. The right column lists personal liabilities, which may include: car loans, home mortgages, credit cards, student debt, etc. Subtracting total liabilities from total assets yields personal or household *net worth* or *net wealth*.

We usually make a distinction between *long-term* assets and liabilities and *short-term* (or *current*) assets and liabilities. Short-term refers to items that mature or come due within one year, while long-term items come due or mature beyond one year in the future.

A balance sheet represents assets, liabilities, and net worth at some specified *point in time*. It is therefore a snapshot representing what you *own* and what you *owe* at that point in time. In contrast, an *income statement* or *budget* shows flows of funds *over a period of time* (More on budgets later). Here's a typical two-column personal balance sheet schema. Dollar amounts have been removed to emphasize just the asset and liability categories.

Personal Balance Sheet Items for: Dr. John Q. Public
March 31, 2017

ASSETS (owned)	LIABILITIES (owed)
SHORT TERM ASSETS cash checking account balances savings account balances money market account balances certificates of deposit (maturity less than one year) other current assets	**SHORT TERM LIABILITIES** credit card balances bank line of credit balances other current liabilities
LONG TERM ASSETS primary residence other real estate owned car(s) furniture jewelry electronic equipment artwork other personal property brokerage/trading accounts retirement accounts (IRA, 401(k)) certificates of deposit (maturity greater than one year) direct business ownership life insurance cash value other long term investments	**LONG TERM LIABILITIES** residence mortgage principal other mortgage principal car loan(s) outstanding home improvement loans student loan balance other long term liabilities

NET WORTH = TOTAL ASSETS – TOTAL LIABILITIES

Since a balance sheet provides a snapshot of your net worth at a particular time, you can track changes in your assets, liabilities and net worth by comparing balance sheets at different time points. For ease of demonstration, I convert the two-column balance sheet into a single-column format, below.

Personal Balance Sheet for: Dr. John Q. Public
(in thousands of dollars, at year-end)

	2015	2016	2017
ASSETS (what you own)			
SHORT TERM ASSETS			
cash	$2	$4	$5
checking account balances	1	3	3
savings account balances	0	3	5
money market account balances	0	0	2
certificates of deposit	0	5	10
(maturity less than one year)			
other current assets	0	0	3
LONG TERM ASSETS			
primary residence	350	360	375
other real estate owned	0	0	110
car(s)	21	19	17
furniture	13	14	15
jewelry	0	2	2
electronic equipment	2	2	2
artwork	0	0	0
other personal property	0	0	0
brokerage/trading accounts	0	0	2
retirement accounts (IRA, 401(k))	45	56	68
certificates of deposit	0	5	10
(maturity greater than one year)			
direct business ownership	0	0	0
life insurance cash value	17	21	25
other long term investments	0	0	0
TOTAL ASSETS (TA)	$451	$493	$654
LIABILITIES (what you owe)			
SHORT TERM LIABILITIES			
credit card balances	4	3	2
bank line of credit balances	10	4	1
other current liabilities	0	0	0
continued on next page ...			

continued on next page ...

LONG TERM LIABILITIES			
residence mortgage principal	280	260	240
other mortgage principal	0	0	0
car loan(s) outstanding	12	11	10
home improvement loans	0	0	0
student loan balance	65	55	45
other long term liabilities	0	0	0
TOTAL LIABILITIES (TL)	**$371**	**$333**	**$298**
NET WORTH (TA-TL)	**$80**	**$160**	**$356**

In this particular example, net worth steadily increases as assets increase and liabilities decrease. This reflects a healthy progression in household assets and liabilities. In reality, many households fail to grow assets (or they increase liabilities as assets increase). Often, such households are not living within their means. Instead, they are over-extended on debt and/or not saving and building up their assets.

Note that some of the entries in the balance sheet are not legitimate pillars because they are not reliable stores of value over the long term. This includes car(s), furniture, electronic equipment and any other property that can be expected to lose value (or depreciate) over time rather than increase in value. Legitimate pillars are *appreciating* assets—those whose value is expected to increase.

When you borrow additional money, your balance sheet *expands*. The amount of the borrowing appears on the right side as more debt, increasing total liabilities. That same amount also appears on the left side, either as cash, or as some new asset, if that's what the borrowing was for (for example, another real estate property). These effects raise total assets. As long as it's affordable for you, using borrowings to gain more appreciating assets is generally a good move—you're collecting more pillars! But if you take the borrowed cash and spend it (an economist would say you 'consume' the cash), you end up wasting it, and simply going more deeply into debt. Your total liabilities will go up while total assets remain the same, and your net worth will decrease. Examples of wasting borrowed money may include throwing unnecessarily lavish parties, gambling, and in some cases, purchasing depreciating assets.

Balance sheets (and all other financial statements for that matter) can be used for forecasting. In the example above, suppose it is early 2018, and you have actual numbers for 2016 and 2017. You can forecast 2018, 2019, and 2020 numbers, and use those to generate net worth forecasts for those same years. If the net worth forecasts look healthy—Congratulations, you're on track! If they're negative or getting smaller over time, you've got a serious problem. In such cases you need to take a closer look at your budget (discussed later) and ensure you are living within your means. This is the only way to reverse these damaging trends.

The Pillars of Wealth Objective

As noted at the beginning of this chapter, your objective should be to: *accumulate as many assets as possible in as many different pillars as possible.* The point in having multiple pillars is to provide diversification. *Diversification* is a risk reduction mechanism which is best summarized by the expression—*don't put all your eggs in one basket.*

Here's a counter example: if all your wealth is in your business (you have no savings elsewhere), and the business fails, say due to a malpractice judgment, you would have no wealth left. In contrast, by spreading your wealth over multiple pillars (or assets), if one suffers a large loss, the other pillars are still there to support your financial needs.

There are several pillars or assets in which we can accumulate wealth. Below are some candidates. Before we get to the actual pillars, I'd like to clarify one question: are pillars the same as asset classes?

Are Pillars the Same as Asset Classes?

You may have noticed that I use the words pillars and assets interchangeably. Both refer to things that have value. The more of these things we own (stocks, bonds, real estate, etc.), the wealthier we are. So pillars and assets can be used interchangeably. Note, however, that pillars are not the same as *asset classes.*

An *asset class* is a collection of assets that share certain risk and return characteristics. The major asset classes are stocks, bonds, and cash equivalents. Real estate is also considered to be an asset class, as are commodities and hedge fund investments (often referred to as 'alternative' asset classes). There are various subcategories of asset classes. For example, stocks may be divided into large company stocks (Large Cap), small company stocks (Small Cap) and emerging market stocks. Bonds may be divided into investment grade (safer) bonds and junk (riskier) bonds. All of these may be subdivided even further, for example, by country or industry. That can get very technical and confusing.

A single pillar may include investments in several asset classes. Our stocks and bonds pillar, in particular, will typically be comprised of Large Cap stocks, Small Cap stocks, emerging market stocks, investment grade bonds, etc. The college savings plan pillar (discussed later) is also likely to include investments in stock and bond asset classes. The real estate pillar (also discussed later) may include investments in our personal home (a retail property asset class) and an investment property leased to a local business (a commercial property asset class).

I prefer to refer to our assets as pillars, as they tend to be more intuitively appealing. We can all relate to needing some cash, saving for college, having an account for stock market investments, buying a home, collecting antiques, etc. We don't need to be mired in the technical jargon of asset classes.

As a practical matter, when you are ready to commit funds to the stock and bond pillar you will invariably make those investments in distinct asset classes. This is because the prepackaged mutual funds and exchange traded funds (ETFs) available to you are generally designed to represent specific asset classes, such as those identified above.

Regardless of whether you prefer to think in terms of asset classes or pillars, the bottom line is that you want to invest in as many different categories (of pillars or asset classes) as possible. If you do this properly you'll end up with a diversified set of assets. As noted above, that is the ultimate objective.

Stocks and Bonds Pillar

Stocks and Bonds are financial securities issued by corporations. Bonds may also be issued by governments. Issuers of stocks and bonds are usually raising money to fund their operations, including expansion plans. For example, a company may raise money to build a specialized factory to produce a medical device, or it may wish to hire new staff to build a global sales team. Government issuers of bonds include those at the federal, state, provincial, or county/city level. A local government may issue bonds to help fund construction of a community center, or a new access road or sewage system.

When corporations issue stocks or bonds they are *raising capital*, where capital is the fancy term economists use instead of simply saying 'money.'

Investing in stocks and bonds allows us to share in the success of the organizations that issued our stocks and bonds. Of course, when those issuers do poorly, we stand to lose money on our investments.

If you invest in only one stock and it does poorly, you could lose your entire investment. Because investing in individual stocks and bonds can be very risky, many investors prefer to invest in portfolios of many stocks or many bonds. This can be done by purchasing pre-constructed portfolios, the most common of these are mutual funds and exchange traded funds (ETFs). Investing in these funds has several advantages: they are more diversified than individual stocks or bonds, and they are convenient. We do, however, pay for this convenience. The companies that put these portfolios together and manage them on an ongoing basis charge us a management fee. This fee is typically a percentage of the amount we invest in a fund, and is expressed as a Management Expense Ratio (MER). So if the MER on a particular fund is 1%, and at the time the fee is assessed the value of your investment in that fund is $40,000, you will be charged $400 dollars annually for that investment. (In practice, the fees are often drawn from your account more frequently, in small amounts. This makes them less noticeable on your statements, thereby reducing the likelihood that you will complain about them).

Mutual fund companies have been implicated over the years in various unsavory marketing and fee–setting practices. For these reasons, and due to their higher fees and lower transparency, mutual funds have been steadily displaced by investments in ETFs.

There's much more to be said about investing. Many books have been written on the subject, including my own reference book titled *Play to Prosper: The Small Investors Survival Guide*. I hope to revise and re-release it as part of the *Pillars of Wealth* series, specifically geared to medical professionals.

In a later chapter, I'll briefly discuss risk and return associated with investments. I'll also cover several account types you can use to invest in stocks and bonds.

Cash Pillar

The word 'cash' is often assumed to mean bills and coins.

In the financial planning world, cash is bills and coins *plus* the contents of a number of other financial accounts. These holdings are sometimes referred to as *cash equivalent instruments*, which include: money in checking and savings accounts, certificates of deposit (CDs), as well as funds in some money market accounts. These are discussed briefly, below.

Liquidity

The unifying feature of money in 'cash' accounts is liquidity. Liquidity is the ability to quickly convert an asset to cash with minimal or no loss in value. Liquidity is an important consideration as it reflects how quickly and easily you can get your hands on money for use on short notice.

Cash Equivalent Instruments

Funds in your checking account are highly liquid. You can access them almost instantaneously. You can go to any ATM and pull out a few hundred dollars. You can go to your bank branch counter and withdraw money immediately. You can also link your Paypal account to your checking account and instantly fund online purchases or transfers.

You can also withdraw money fairly quickly from savings accounts. But there's a difference between savings and checking accounts. Technically, the bank can choose to make you wait anywhere from a couple of days to a month before giving you money from your savings account.

Banks have no reason to create ill will with their clients, so they usually allow you to make savings account transactions quickly and seamlessly. But the bank is within its rights to delay withdrawals from savings accounts.

Money in a certificate of deposit (CD) can be accessed quickly, but there may be a redemption penalty equal to some percentage of the interest earned on the CD. This reduces the liquidity benefit of CDs. But we can still consider them to be cash equivalents since they can be redeemed on short notice (with relatively minor interest penalties).

Money market accounts may also be considered similar to cash as long as we are allowed to withdraw funds from them without penalties. For this reason we exclude money market funds which are offered through qualified accounts, e.g., 401(k)s, because hefty penalties may apply to withdrawals. For example, say you need to repair the roof on your home or buy a new car. If you elect to withdraw funds from a 401(k) account, you may have to pay taxes on the amount withdrawn *and* an additional 10% penalty.

Now compare the relative liquidity of our cash equivalents to investments in real estate. Real estate is on the other end of the liquidity spectrum. We could say that real estate is *illiquid*. It may take months to sell real estate, and if you have to sell quickly, you can only do so by reducing the price dramatically, undermining the asset's value.

Readily available cash is crucial to cover expected and unexpected expenses. If you don't have available cash to cover immediate obligations, you may have to liquidate investment assets (as in the real estate example, above). This disrupts the intended investment and may result in severe penalties or value losses.

Resorting to the use of credit cards to cover expenses is another danger, as it may obligate you to carry a large balance with a punishingly high interest rate (on the order of 20% to 25% annually).

The safest path is to always have some cash on hand to cover unexpected expenses.

Rainy Day Fund

Think of cash you set aside as a *rainy day* (or emergency) fund. You can draw money as needed from the fund, without disrupting your long-term financial planning, or having to use credit cards.

A common recommendation is to amass a rainy day fund equivalent to between 3 to 6 months of *non-discretionary* expenses. Non-discretionary means expenses you're committed to making— That is, expenses you *cannot* avoid.

The idea is that if your finances become constrained you would respond by cutting back on discretionary (*unnecessary*) expenses, leaving you with enough money to cover 3-6 months of *necessary* expenses.

An alternative rule of thumb is to have an emergency fund equivalent to 6 months' salary. So if your gross monthly salary is twelve thousand dollars, you would hold total cash and cash equivalents (checking, savings, CDs, and money market accounts) amounting to about seventy-two thousand dollars (twelve thousand times 6).

A Roth IRA is viewed by some as a substitute or complementary rainy day fund. Roth IRA contributions are made with post-tax dollars, which means money on which you've already paid tax. So you can withdraw your *contributions* without penalties. You may, however, be required to pay taxes and/or penalties on any earnings (or gains) generated in the account and withdrawn prematurely. Keep in mind that it may take some time (a week or more) to receive those early withdrawals, making them somewhat less effective for true emergency situations. More importantly, Roth IRAs have very favorable tax advantages, so you don't want to prematurely withdraw funds from them if you can avoid it. I'll say more about Roth IRAs later in this book.

Where Does the 3-6 Month Guideline Come From?

There's no deep science behind the 3-6 month guideline for your rainy day fund. If you lose your job it may take you somewhere between 3 to 6 months to find another. If you become disabled, it may take you 3-6 months to recover and return to work, or until your long-term disability policy is triggered and begins to pay you benefits.

Why Not Hold More Than 6 Months Salary?

If having more cash or liquid assets is good, why not hold more than 6 months of salary or non-discretionary expenses? To arrive at the answer, we first need to observe that the more liquid an asset, the lower its return. The most liquid form of cash is, of course, coins and bills.

How much interest do you receive for holding physical cash?

Zero!

What about the next most liquid category? How much interest do you receive on your checking account?

Effectively zero!

What about Savings accounts?

A very small amount, generally less than one or two percent. During periods of very low interest rates, savings accounts may pay interest of 0.3%, or less, annually.

To get higher returns you must take more risk. One risk you can take is liquidity risk. You can obtain higher interest or return by investing in low liquidity investments (such as real estate).

So the answer to the original question is that you can hold more assets in cash and cash equivalents, but those assets aren't working for you. They're not helping you to grow your wealth, because the returns they offer are very low. To reach your financial goals you want as much of your money as possible to be productive. Cash is safe, but it's not very productive.

That's why we invest our money in stocks, bonds, and real estate. Because we want and need those higher returns to grow our pillars to a point where they can support our financial needs, including retirement.

I have a relative who is a very accomplished physician. He's so distrustful of financial advisors that he decided to keep all his money in a checking account. For several years his checking account balance was over $300,000, and eventually rose to $500,000. While we can all sympathize with his distrust of advisors, he could (and really should) have placed most of this money in higher yielding assets. At the very least, he could have put the money in government insured CDs, earning a few percent a year to keep up with inflation. Instead, he was effectively giving his bank an interest-free loan!

Real Estate Pillar

Your real estate pillar of wealth typically begins with your home, assuming you own it. Over time, you may add properties to your real estate portfolio. Additions may include a second home, and potentially rental properties rented to other families or businesses.

Home Ownership

Opting to buy a primary residence (your home) is a non-trivial consideration. Yes, it yields a pillar of wealth, but it also saddles you with long-term financial responsibilities and legal liability as a property owner.

Home ownership is appealing for several reasons, including:

- Real estate is tangible, it's real—we can touch it and know it's there
- While real estate can decline in value, it's generally a reliable long-term appreciating asset
- Real estate can be a decent defense against inflation (although it's not as perfect a defense as some people think)
- There may be favorable mortgage interest deductions for homeowners

In the Managing Debt chapter of this book I discuss: the downsides of owning a home, the buy vs. rent decision, home equity lines of credit, and the implications of missing a mortgage payment.

Real Estate as an Investment

In addition to (or instead of) owning your own home, you can purchase a property as an investment and rent it to others. Here are some reasons to consider real estate as an investment:

- Capital Gain – Capital gain is the difference between the prices at which you buy and sell the property. You don't pay capital gains taxes until you sell the property, so there's an element of tax deferral in real estate investment
- Tax Deductions – many rental property-related expenses are deductible, allowing you to reduce your tax obligation.

Examples may include: property taxes, management fees, repair and maintenance costs, and mortgage interest payments

- Depreciation – you can depreciate a percentage of the property value from rental income each year. This reduces your tax bill in that year

- Accumulating Equity – the tenant's rent payments help you to pay off your mortgage and steadily build equity in the property. Due to the structure of amortization schedules, most of the early monthly payments go toward interest, with only a small fraction going toward reducing the principal (and building equity). But as each month and year goes by, more of each payment goes toward paying the principal, and equity buildup accelerates. (As this shift from interest to principal occurs, your allowed interest deductions may decrease)

- Cash Flow – when your income from a property is consistently greater than all expenses on the property, it is said to generate 'positive cash flow.' You can direct this cash flow into retirement accounts or accumulate it until there's enough to make a down payment on another property

Successful real estate investors do a good job identifying properties that can yield solid positive cash flow, and use those flows to purchase a portfolio of properties. Once you reach a critical mass of properties, you can attain some economies of scale and control your expenses even further. For example, when you own only one rental property you may have to pay a plumber a large amount for each service call. But with ten properties you can strike a deal with a local plumber to take care of all your properties at more favorable rates. The same goes for all maintenance personnel (electricians, landscapers, tree experts, etc.).

Being a Landlord Isn't for Everyone

It's easy to get caught up in the excitement of making a passive income through real estate, but it's not as glamorous as it seems. Many people, after learning hard lessons, decide this isn't for them.

Some of those downsides:

- If you're buying property with a view to renting it to others, you take on all the landlord headaches. Your phone may ring in the middle of the night with complaints from your tenant about an overflowing toilet, broken appliance, or flooded basement. Do you really want to have to take those calls?

- As a landlord, you rely on monthly rents to pay a mortgage. Whenever the property is vacant, you have to cover those mortgage payments yourself. This can be a heavy strain on your household finances

- Tenants may cause damage to a property and/or they may refuse to pay rent, forcing you to go through an emotionally painful and financially expensive eviction process

Before becoming a landlord, carefully consider the anticipated expenditures, headaches, and distractions.

Direct Business Ownership Pillar

This refers to significant ownership stakes in sole proprietorships, partnerships, and corporations. An obvious example is your private practice—assuming you have one. Other examples may be a stake you've taken in a bio-tech or other start-up company, or ownership of a family business you may have inherited.

The second book in the *Pillars of Wealth* series, *Finance and Business Essentials for Medical Practices*, addresses private practice ownership in detail.

The Small Business Administration (SBA.gov) offers a lot of useful information for small business owners. One of the most important early decisions is how to structure your business. The SBA provides useful summaries of business structure alternatives, along with their relative advantages and disadvantages.

Business ownership is complex. It requires new skill sets. These include technical skills such as accounting and finance, as well as people management skills. In the Information Age, it's also increasingly critical to understand social networking solutions. These are necessary for you to find patients and for them to find you.

A typical scenario for doctors who own a practice is that much of their wealth is tied up in the business. This means they have just one single, concentrated pillar. It's highly advisable, for diversification purposes, to gradually draw value out of the business and invest it in other pillars. The simple logic is that if all your wealth is in the practice, and it fails—for whatever reason—you could be left with very little to support your family and your retirement.

College Savings Pillar

There are many ways to facilitate saving for college. It's easy to find information on the various offerings online. We'll focus on 529 plans, which have become the most popular savings mechanisms specifically focused on education.

A 529 plan is a tax-advantaged investment program designed to facilitate savings for higher education expenses. 529 Plans are formally known as "Qualified Tuition Programs." Plans are administered at the state level and come in two forms: prepaid tuition and college savings plans.

According to the CollegeSavings.org website, *Prepaid Tuition Plans* (sometimes called guaranteed savings plans) allow participants to pre-purchase future tuition at a predetermined rate today. Typically, an account owner will purchase somewhere between one and four years of tuition for a young child. When that child reaches college age, the plan pays out based on tuition rates at that time.

College Savings Plans are different in that your account earnings are directly based on the market performance of underlying investments. Those investments are typically in mutual funds. Most 529 savings plans offer age-based investment options. Their underlying investments become more conservative as the beneficiary gets closer to college-age. More specifically, their asset mix changes over time from a heavier weighting on stocks to a heavier weighting on less volatile securities—namely bonds. They also offer static investment options where the underlying investments remain in the same fund or combination of funds regardless of the beneficiary's age.

Investment choices in 529 plan accounts tend to be limited to a small set of funds. These are directly managed by the state or an investment manager contracted by the state. By law, you're allowed to make changes to your investment choices up to twice a year. There are ongoing efforts to increase this frequency.

You can choose to invest in your state's plan, or in a plan offered by another state. The CollegeSavings.org site allows you to compare plans.

Tax-Related Benefits

Money in a 529 plan grows tax deferred. The money may be withdrawn tax-free when used for qualified higher education expenses. Such expenses include: tuition, mandatory fees, room and board, books, school supplies, and required equipment.

Many states offer additional tax deductions, credits, or other benefits to residents enrolled in their own state's program.

What If My Child Doesn't Go to College?

The plan beneficiary may be changed to any of a number of eligible family members. These include: another child or stepchild, a first cousin, niece or nephew, other generations of the family, as well as the spouses of all eligible family members.

If there's no alternative beneficiary and you wish to gain access to the funds for non-educational purposes, you can withdraw them from the 529. But, you must pay state and federal taxes, plus a 10% federal penalty on any earnings withdrawn. Your original contributions are made after tax, so they're generally not subject to these taxes and penalties.

What If My Child Gets a Scholarship?

Funds in the plan could be applied to any other eligible higher education expenses not covered by the scholarship. Unused earnings withdrawn from the plan would be subject to taxation at the scholarship winner's tax rate but the 10% penalty would not apply.

Overall Household Portfolio Diversification

529 plans invested in stock or bond funds may exhibit similar risk and return characteristics to investments in your retirement or brokerage accounts. If so, your 529 plan investments may not deliver

much diversification across your other pillars. That is, since 529s and your retirement assets are often invested in similar holdings, declines in your 529 account are unlikely to be offset by increases in other investment assets (e.g., in a brokerage account or IRA). You can, of course, purposely select investments in your various accounts that increase the scope for diversification.

This point about diversification does not negate the significant tax benefits of saving for college. So, a 529 plan will likely be a useful addition to your pillars.

Insurance Cash Value Pillar

This section focuses only on the cash value feature of permanent life insurance policies. A much more detailed discussion of these (often controversial) policies is provided in a later chapter.

A portion of each permanent insurance premium payment you make goes to pay: government taxes, the overhead costs of the insurance company, and the actuarial cost of insurance. Any remaining amounts of each premium contribute to building up cash value. Cash value in a policy belongs to the policy owner. Funds in cash value accounts accumulate on a tax deferred basis.

Cash value accounts accrue interest over time and the insurer also has the discretion to pay dividends on some policy types, for example, Whole Life. The policy owner can choose whether to withdraw those dividends or keep them in the account where they can help cash value to build faster.

In addition to being a repository of value in its own right (a pillar), the cash value account can diversify other pillars or investments (for example, in stocks and bonds).

Cash value grows relatively slowly in early years. For some policies, it may take an entire decade before any meaningful amount of cash value is accumulated.

In some situations, life insurance cash value may be protected from creditors (depending on state-specific laws).

Is Life Insurance Cash Value an Investment?

Critics of permanent life insurance policies often point out that insurance cash value accumulation compares unfavorably with investments in stocks and bonds. While my sympathies generally lie with the critics, it's important to remain intellectually honest. Technically, a non-variable life insurance policy (for example, Whole Life) is not an investment. Rather, it's more accurate to describe it as having a *savings* feature.

This doesn't stop some agents from implying that permanent policies are investments in an effort to make them seem more appealing to consumers. Since such policies are not investments, there's not much point in comparing their returns to those expected from stocks. Insurance policies will invariably seem inferior in such examinations, but these are not true apples-to-apples comparisons. Additional details regarding this controversial topic are provided in the Insurance chapter.

Whole Life Policies offer some interest rate guarantees. As a result, cash value accumulation in such policies is fairly stable. In contrast, cash value accumulation in variable policies such as Variable Life and Indexed Life may be quite volatile.

Annuities Pillar

An annuity is a two-phase contract between an investor (you) and a financial institution (typically an insurance company). The contract states that in the first phase, known as the *accumulation* phase, you will make periodic payments for a specified period of time (for example, 20 years), to the insurance company.

In the case of a *fixed* annuity, your contributions grow at a fixed, agreed-upon, contractual rate. In the case of a *variable* annuity, your growth rate depends on the performance of underlying investments.

Instead of making periodic payments, you can also fund an annuity by making a single, lump sum contribution.

The second phase is known as the *payout* phase. During this phase the direction of cash flows is reversed. Now, you receive distributions from the insurance company. You have several payout alternatives:

- Cash out your entire lump sum of accumulated funds
- Receive a stream of constant distributions over an agreed-upon period of time
- Receive constant payments until you die

Annuities are typically priced based on your life expectancy. So they can provide solid returns if you live longer than expected. This is because you'll receive more payments from the insurance company over more years. On the other hand, if you die prematurely, you (or your beneficiaries) may end up on the short end.

In the case of a variable annuity, you may receive variable payments over time based on the performance of the underlying investments. Variable annuities may provide a guaranteed minimum payout, for example, 1%, but it may be much lower than a fixed annuity's payout.

In some states, annuities may receive some protection from creditors. Make sure you know the laws in your state.

Tax Considerations

Contributions during the accumulation period are generally not tax deductible. But the funds in the account do grow tax deferred. You're generally required to pay taxes on the earned income component of distributions. You don't pay taxes on the contributions themselves, since these were made after tax.

Surrender Charges

Annuities can have very onerous *surrender charges*. These are the penalties you must pay if you want to terminate the annuity agreement before the contractual date. Generally, surrender charges gradually decline until they phase out completely over time. But you may have to own the annuity for ten years before the phasing out is complete. That's a long time. So when you purchase an annuity, you must view it as a long term move.

Since you're going to be invested for a long time, you want some assurance that the seller of the annuity will be around for the long term. I discuss identifying good insurance companies later, in the insurance chapter.

Susceptibility to Inflation

Fixed annuities are especially vulnerable to inflation. This is not unique to annuities. The vulnerability is shared by most fixed income products, including many bonds and bond funds. To diversify some of that exposure, you could *annuitize* (convert into a stream of payments) just a fraction of your accumulated nest egg. Keep the rest in reserve, invested in other, diversifying assets. You can always annuitize more of the remaining nest egg later to create more predictable income. Annuitizing *after* rates have gone up should allow you to qualify for higher payout rates.

Riders (Extra Features)

You can purchase annuities with a variety of *riders* (or extra features). Examples: Some riders may guarantee your principal. Others may guarantee a growth rate for your accumulating funds. And yet others may guarantee a death benefit to your beneficiaries. Annuities can get very complicated. Adding riders often adds even more confusion, and you have to pay for them. My experience with riders is that they often cost more than they're worth. Many consumers conclude that annuities, in general, cost more than they're worth.

Problems with Annuities

There are some very significant problems with annuities. They often have:

- Exorbitant fees
- High surrender charges
- Opaque calculations
- Unnecessary complexity

Some annuities are so complex that even insurance agents don't fully understand them. This is particularly the case with variable annuities.

While the annuity industry today deserves much criticism, on paper, guaranteed or fixed annuities can make a lot of sense. They allow you to build up a nest egg on a tax deferred basis, and later to turn it into a predictable lifetime income stream. This can be very useful for financial planning purposes, giving annuities a role as legitimate pillars of wealth.

There are some encouraging signs. Insurance companies are interested in shedding expensive agent networks that tend to contribute to reputational risks and legal liability. Increasingly, we're seeing more companies shaking up the *status quo* by offering commoditized and transparent direct-sold annuities. These bypass expensive and potentially unscrupulous salesmen. Increasing competition may help drive the industry in a new direction, with simpler, cheaper, more standardized annuity products sold directly to consumers. Given consumer sentiment there's reason to believe this change will happen. When it does, we should be ready to embrace such tools rather than being reflexively biased against them.

Currently, however, annuities are often more trouble than they're worth. This applies especially to variable annuities.

For some households, annuities may make sense, but even in those cases, I suggest small exposures that complement existing pillar allocations, rather than large allocations to annuities that may be susceptible to unfair fees and inflation.

Collectibles Pillar

Some collectibles—such as art, coins, stamps, sports memorabilia, antiques, and vintage cars—have significant monetary value. Collections of these items are therefore also potential pillars. Of course, the value of collectibles can vary over time, and may depend heavily on changes in supply and demand. Supply and demand may be affected by various factors, including: overall economic conditions, demographic changes, and consumer preferences.

This means that the value of such collections must be estimated very carefully in the financial planning process to ensure it is realistic. This is my subtle way of trying to convince you that your retro video game, or shot glass collection from college may not be a guaranteed path to retirement.

In my experience, valuable collections are usually created by doctors *after* they begin to generate significant earnings. This means that owning a collectibles pillar is more likely to happen when you're older, more established, and have the disposable excess funds to spend on mainstream collectibles such as artwork or antiques. Another path to owning a valuable collection is to inherit it. (Inheritance is discussed in the next section).

If you do own a legitimate collection with objectively verifiable value you must, of course, protect it. This entails expenditures on insurance and in some cases on building the appropriate storage infrastructure. For example, valuable stamps or artwork must be stored in temperature, light, and humidity controlled environments.

If you like to display your collection, you need space. This can mean dedicating an entire room to an antique book collection, or a large garage to house your selection of antique cars.

For many people, collecting isn't about commercial gain. It's about emotional fulfillment and satisfaction. Often that comes from the beauty or sentimental appeal of the items in the collection. The mere suggestion of selling all or part of a collection to fund retirement may result in a strong negative reaction.

So, collectibles can be a legitimate pillar as long as they have real value *and* the owner is comfortable with realizing that value through a sale.

Anticipated Inheritance Pillar

If you have a parent or relative who has promised you an inheritance, you're the potential recipient of a free pillar of wealth. But until that money actually arrives, it's still a potential—but not guaranteed—source of wealth. This is because despite the best intentions, the generous benefactor may outlive his money. He may squander it recklessly in a gambling establishment. Or, he may decide he no longer likes you, or your spouse, or your children, and may amend the Will to exclude you.

Even if a relative promises and delivers some inheritance, you may not have any certainty in advance regarding the size of that inheritance. So while you may feel secure with the expectation of an inheritance, you should avoid relying on it as your sole pillar of wealth.

For the sake of conservatism, I recommend ignoring such anticipated pillars entirely during financial planning.

As the estate transfer date looms closer (for example, due to a surviving parent's ailing health) it's helpful for everyone to ensure the most painless transfer of ownership. Ideally, your family (including the parent leaving the inheritance and siblings sharing in it) are able to discuss this *openly*. It may be too much to say that you can discuss it *comfortably*.

Financial considerations often take a distant back seat when you're concerned about the health of your sole surviving parent. Nevertheless, an estate can be left in various states of disrepair. Simple logic suggests that an estate with proper planning will take less money, time, and headaches to transfer to the next generation.

You may wish to review the Estate Planning chapter presented later in this book. Instead of applying the content from your perspective as the one disposing of assets, view your parent as the one in that position. To facilitate the conversation it may be helpful to share the chapter with your parent.

The bottom line is that everyone benefits from a smooth process. It allows you to focus on living life to the fullest with your aging parents and having the time to grieve properly when they're no longer there.

Despite the obvious logic, it can be difficult to initiate this conversation with a parent. We don't want to come across as being motivated by greed, as in "So, what are you leaving me in your Will?" But the conversation needs to take place. It may be helpful to initiate the talk by saying something like: "It's going to be very difficult for me to deal with losing you. I don't want to be faced with estate-related questions at the same time. There are lots of guides on how to plan properly. Let's sit down this weekend and work through one of them."

In most cases, I expect your parent will be relieved to hear this. He or she most likely wants to get this done but has found it awkward to begin the conversation

Precarious Pillars

I now turn my attention to pillars which are, for a variety of reasons, less reliable. I'll cover three such precarious pillars: Social Security, Pension Plans, and Anticipated Lottery Winnings.

Social Security

Social Security Benefits are available to most American workers, with the exception of some state and local government employees. Currently, those who work and pay Social Security taxes can earn credits toward Social Security benefits. A total of 40 credits are required to qualify for retirement benefits. This is equivalent to working and contributing for at least 10 years. The more you contribute and the longer you contribute, the more you are eligible to receive in retirement years. You should be aware that the currently advertized maximum monthly benefit amounts are *not* sufficient to maintain a middle income life style.

With increased life expectancies and the baby boomer retirement wave, the Social Security program's ability to pay benefits to retirees has been, and will continue to be, severely strained. The safest approach for those who have enough other income is to ignore any expected social security benefits during retirement planning.

This is not practical for many workers who desperately rely on Social Security benefits to make ends meet. But if you can afford to ignore social security—you'll be better prepared. The logic is obvious: if you ignore social security in your planning, and the program is severely cut back, your financial plans and retirement will not suffer. If Social Security survives, that added income will be a welcome bonus. The alternative—relying on Social Security only to see it collapse—is a bad strategic move.

The Social Security website (www.ssa.gov) has a lot of useful information, including calculators to estimate your life expectancy and your benefits in retirement.

Pension Plans

There are two types of retirement plans: defined benefit and defined contribution.

A *defined benefit plan* is one in which retirees know in advance what their benefits will be. Pension benefits are *defined* based on the number of years an employee has been employed by the organization and her salary history. Qualification for these plans requires long-term commitment to an employer, often on the order of ten years. Once eligible, an employee is promised a steady pension income stream in retirement. Decades ago, America's largest companies offered extremely generous versions of these pension plans. This made them expensive to maintain. For this reason, over recent decades many organizations have greatly scaled back or ended defined benefit plans in favor of defined contribution plans.

Defined contribution plans involve defined (or specified) *contributions* to retirement accounts, but no guaranteed benefits. This category includes 401(k) and 403(b) accounts, in which the employee decides what her contributions will be each year. Employers may contribute some matching funds to employees' plans. At retirement, employees begin withdrawing the funds that have accumulated in their plans. The total accumulated in an employee's fund depends entirely on how much that employee contributed, and what he decided to invest in. If investments turn out to be unsuccessful, there's less available to that employee in retirement. The employer bears no responsibility for the investment choices made by employees.

Traditional defined benefit pension plans create potentially large obligations for companies, as they're responsible for delivering the defined pension benefits to retirees. Such obligations have brought some firms near, or all the way to, bankruptcy. Companies that completely collapse may not be able to honor their pension liabilities.

I'm not suggesting that defined benefit pension plans are doomed to fail. It's possible that you've earned very generous and reliable pension benefits. That's a good thing. Those benefits may be too large to ignore in your planning. There's nothing wrong with that.

I just want to make you aware of the bigger picture. Because the future of Social Security and defined benefit pension plans may be precarious, I recommend omitting them from your planning, if possible. This is the most conservative approach. As noted earlier, in the event either of these provides you with meaningful cash flow in retirement, you'll be ahead of the game.

Anticipated Lottery Winnings

This is only partly a joke—some people are sustained by the false belief that lottery winnings will materialize and cover all their future financial needs. But a realist understands that you can't sit back and hope, or pray, for assets to magically appear in retirement.

You need to get them the old fashioned way, by building them carefully through hard work and prudent consideration of risk and return.

Diversified Pillars

I've already talked about diversification, but this concept is sufficiently important to warrant a few more observations.

Many doctors reach retirement age with one large pillar. That single pillar may be:

1. A retirement account such as a 401(k), 403(b), or IRA, containing several million dollars, or
2. A medical practice servicing hundreds of loyal patients that is worth several million dollars

The danger when you only have one major pillar is that if it's damaged, for whatever reason, your entire financial foundation may be devastated. The basic defense against a single vulnerable pillar is to have many pillars.

Individual pillars are not just susceptible to economic forces. They can also be undermined by legislative changes. There was recently a legislative effort underway to cap the cumulative amount of contributions made into retirement accounts. While it's unclear whether this will become law, it's prudent to think ahead about diversifying. Perhaps the most important message here is that even the most sacred of cows we rely on for decades can be taken away from us. As baby boomers retire *en masse,* and our public safety nets get stretched to the breaking point, it's wise to recognize that more of the tools we rely on for retirement, including tax breaks, will come under fire. Since we don't know which assets may be most disadvantaged in future, our best move is to diversify our holdings across as many assets or pillars as possible.

Where Do The Pillars Come From?

We've discussed multiple pillars of wealth, but we haven't yet explained where these pillars actually come from?

Money doesn't magically appear in your retirement accounts; a home doesn't build and pay for itself; your medical practice isn't established by divine edict.

With the exception of an inheritance or winning the lottery, *all your pillars of wealth are enabled by your human capital*—everything is made possible by your education, expertise, and hard work.

As a young professional, it may seem difficult to quantify the value of this human capital, but there is real value there. Everything depends on your ability to continue with your career and realize your earning potential (i.e., monetize your hard-won education and expertise).

It should be clear that you must protect your human capital, as your pillars will never come to be if disability or death disrupts your career. Carefully selected disability and life insurance policies can be used to safe-guard your human capital value. Purchasing such insurance ensures that in the event of your death or disability, your family or estate will be endowed with valuable pillars: a cash pillar with an income-tax-free lump sum death benefit or a pillar with a value equivalent to the sum of many years' worth of disability benefits. Insurance policies are discussed in greater detail in the Insurance chapter.

Credential Management

Your human capital enables all your professional and financial achievements. You build human capital by attending medical or dental school, completing a residency and/or fellowship, working in a hospital or private practice, performing procedures in your specialty area, leveraging affiliations with other professionals in groups or hospitals, and any other experiences you are exposed to during your career.

Hospitals have to confirm these accomplishments (your credentials) in order to approve you for patient admission privileges while insurance companies will require your credentials prior to approving you for payments.

This means you need to retain the paperwork associated with milestones such as: attending medical or dental or pharmacy school, completing a residency, passing licensing exams, performing procedures, etc. Items you should keep in your records include letters and certificates confirming board certifications, licenses, degrees, completion of continuing education courses, start and end dates of all jobs, quality reports listing all procedures you've completed at each position, as well as (favorable) job references. The guiding rule here is: *if in doubt, keep it.*

For the most part, electronic record keeping of credentials hasn't quite made it into the 21st century. This is a problem in that the archaic way credentials are tracked and verified by employers and insurance companies means lengthy and frustrating delays, especially if any red flags are raised.

Dr. Dipan Desai, MD, a former colleague at Johns Hopkins University, recommends staying in touch with administrators at your former training institutions. This makes it easier to pick up the phone and request a letter to confirm your attendance and completion of internship, residency, and fellowship.

According to Michael Simmons, founder of the startup credentials management firm CredSimple, an unexplained gap in employment of more than three months will raise a red flag with insurers or employers. This doesn't mean you won't be approved or hired, but you may be asked about it during an interview, and it could delay your approval. It can normally take as many as two to three months for an employer (a hospital) to obtain appropriate approvals for a new physician's credentials. It can then take up to another two to three months to obtain appropriate status with all relevant insurers. The last thing you need is to create further delays due to gaps in your employment history or a simple error in your reported graduation date (which according to Simmons, could lead to rejection of your application). You can help your own cause by keeping good records throughout your career, and making them available to expedite the credentialing process.

A *New England Journal of Medicine* article authored by Cutler, Wikler and Basch (2012) states that

> *Credentialing and other systems that are used to establish contracts between providers and health plans are riddled with redundancy, with many organizations collecting virtually identical information from providers. The typical physician spends more than 3 hours annually submitting nearly 18 different credentialing forms, with staff spending an additional 20 hours.*

And these procedures must be repeated every one to two years by hospitals and every three years by insurance companies.

Clearly, anything you and your support staff can do to reduce time spent on credential management means more time for patient care. And I haven't said a word yet about the financial cost of these approvals, which can run from $250 to $800 per application. With allied health care professionals (nurse practitioners and physician assistants) being pushed to perform more procedures for cost-cutting reasons, their qualifications and credentials are also subject to increasing scrutiny.

While the existing credentialing system is costly and frustrating, it's the only line of defense ensuring that those providing services to patients are properly qualified. Do yourself and your employer a favor and maintain all relevant human capital records in an organized and easily accessible fashion.

Pillar of Strength – Your Spouse or Partner

To paraphrase the old saying, *behind every great doctor is a doctor's great spouse*. The prosperity of your household depends not just on your human capital. It also depends critically on your *significant other's* human capital. Whether your spouse is a bread winner or homemaker, his or her contributions to the family directly impact everyone's success, including yours.

There are at least three immediate implications to this observation:

1. Collaborate with your spouse when making decisions – Most relationship problems have to do with money. Reconciling your perspectives and working towards the same goals makes for a much smoother and more stable home life
2. Protect your spouse – Make sure your spouse carries appropriate insurance coverage
3. Nurture your spouse – This recommendation is self-evident (and a bit beyond the scope of this book). Your happiness is intricately linked to the happiness of your family unit

The thrust of all this is that a relationship based on genuine affection and mutual respect is one you can rely on for the long term. It's an important pillar of stability throughout your life.

Investing Basics & Account Types

All forms of investment (in stocks, bonds, real estate, etc.) are undertaken with the objective of obtaining some positive reward or return. We recognize that in seeking these rewards, we must face various risks. The aforementioned investments specifically expose us to what is known as *Speculative Risk*.

According to Investopedia:

> *Speculative risk is a category of risk that, when undertaken, results in an uncertain degree of gain or loss. All speculative risks are made as conscious choices and are not just a result of uncontrollable circumstances.*

In other words, we consciously choose to take on speculative risk, motivated by potential upside or financial gain. (Later in this book we will encounter a different kind of risk, known as *pure risk*).

Strictly speaking, because returns from stock and most bond investments are uncertain, we refer to them as *expected* returns or *expected* gains. We can increase the expected return by taking on a more risky investment or we can decrease the expected return through a lower risk investment.

For example, high yield bonds, as the name implies, offer higher yields or expected returns than investment grade bonds. The former are issued by firms with low creditworthiness and hence higher risk, while the latter are issued by firms with more stable prospects. Alternatively, stocks issued by very small firms are generally riskier than stocks issued by much larger and more established corporations.

Investments in the former are expected to provide a higher return than investments in the latter.

A crucial observation is that your investment decisions (and more broadly—all financial decisions) *must simultaneously take into account both risk and return*. A common error is to become overly concerned about risk to the point that you're passing on investments with a favorable risk-return tradeoff. Another common error is to be so swayed or seduced by promises of high returns that you ignore or downplay the risks.

Investment Strategies

Broadly speaking, there are two investment strategies available to you: active investing and passive investing

An *active investing strategy* is all about searching for undervalued securities (usually stocks). Active investing requires in-depth analysis and leads to more frequent trading, both of which lead to higher fees for investors. Frequent selling can also trigger tax obligations.

A *passive investing strategy* strives to mimic a well-defined index of stocks such as the S&P 500® (a portfolio of large firms listed in the United States). Passive investments require no in-depth analysis, incur fewer trading costs and have lower management fees. They also tend to trigger fewer taxable events.

A common analogy for distinguishing these two strategies is to say that active investing is all about expending resources (time, money, analysis) on finding the few needles in the haystack that may outperform the market average. In contrast, passive investing is like saying: *I don't want to spend all that time and energy and money on finding the needles in the haystack (and likely getting some of them wrong anyway). Instead, I'll just buy the entire haystack.*

The most extreme version of active investing is investing in hedge funds. Many people are overawed by the apparent glamour of hedge funds. But the reality of hedge fund investments for most investors is summarized below:

> ... *there are now nearly eight thousand hedge funds, and on average they have underperformed the stock market for nine of the past ten years.* – James Surowiecki, *The New Yorker*, June 10, 2013

The point is that while active investing strategies seem glamorous and profitable, most people are better off avoiding the volatility associated with them.

Lots of money managers want our money and will go to great lengths to convince us that they're the geniuses who can find the next big winners. They insist they're the only ones who can deliver mind-blowing returns. They show us fancy presentations and secret-looking white papers arguing that their trading rules work. Sometimes they make us sign non-disclosure agreements that make us believe they really have something of value.

What does it mean when a mutual fund company shows us a track record of market outperformance over five years? Does it mean the investment can be expected to outperform consistently in future? — No! But our human brains insist this is unusual and 'compelling' evidence. We forget that luck alone predicts that some funds will do better over five years while others do worse. Keep in mind that most fund companies manage dozens of mutual funds. At any given time they will advertise that subset of their funds that has performed well, while quietly ignoring (or closing) those that performed poorly.

Much research has shown that the average investor is better off sticking with a passive strategy. It takes less time and effort, comes at lower cost, and allows us to focus on other priorities.

Investment Account Types

In this section I discuss several account types or plans you can use to manage your stock and bond investments. These investment accounts are distinguished by their tax-related characteristics, ranging from significant tax benefits to no tax benefits at all.

Qualified Retirement Plans

Qualified retirement plans are typically sponsored by an employer. Common examples are 401(k) and 403(b) plans. Hospitals often offer 403(b) plans to employees. If you own a medical practice, you may elect to make a 401(k) plan available to your employees.

The plans become *qualified* by meeting IRS guidelines, which in turn allows them to provide tax advantages to the sponsor (employer) and the employee. Typically, employees can choose (subject to some limits) what percentage of their salary they wish to contribute annually to their accounts. Employers may offer to match employee contributions up to a certain limit, for example, 6% of their salary.

Employers can deduct their contributions from corporate earnings, leading to tax savings for the corporation. Employees can contribute to these plans with pre-tax dollars, reducing their taxable income for that year. Gains within the plans are tax deferred, which means that no taxes are due until the employee begins to receive distributions from the account. The prevailing logic is that distributions will be received when the account holder is retired, at which time her tax rate will be lower than when she was employed.

There are rules governing how much can be contributed per year, when distributions must be taken from such accounts and how much must be taken each year. Taking distributions prior to age 59½ may trigger a 10% penalty, on top of the taxes payable on the amount withdrawn. The 2016 limit on your annual 401(k) or 403(b) tax deferred contributions is $18,000. The IRS refers to this as your *Elective Deferral* amount. If you're over the age of 50, you're allowed an extra $6,000 (known as a *catch-up* contribution). The total *Defined Contribution Limit* for 2016 (the combined amount you and your employer can contribute) is $53,000. It's anticipated that 2017 limits will either remain the same or increase slightly. I suggest you check the IRS website for the latest updates (www.irs.gov).

Vesting

When an employer contributes matching funds to your retirement account, those funds may not automatically become your property. The employer may impose a *vesting* schedule, which specifies when each amount contributed by the employer legally becomes your property. Any amount that has been *vested* is yours. When you leave that firm you can take any vested amounts with you, usually by rolling funds over into an Individual Retirement Account (or IRA). Any amounts which have not yet vested when you leave an employer revert back to the employer.

Vesting schedules vary. Some examples are: (1) Vesting occurs after three years (each contribution made by the employer vests only after three full years have passed and the employee is still working at the company), or (2) 25% of each employer contribution vests each year, so each matching amount becomes fully vested after a total of four years, again assuming you're still an employee.

Your own contributions and any gains on your contributions are always immediately fully vested to you.

The money contributed (by both employee and employer) into these plans is typically invested in mutual funds (portfolios of stocks and bonds). Management of qualified accounts is often undertaken by a financial institution. It may offer its own mutual funds or allow you to choose funds managed by other companies. Generally, there's a limited choice of funds in 401(k) and 403(b) plans. For example, you may have to choose from only ten or fewer funds. This is bad for you as it limits your ability to diversify.

Often, employees accept the default settings on these accounts. Default settings may invest your contributions in mutual funds with unnecessarily high fees. Look closely at the available choices and direct your contributions to the most advantageous investments, which often means those with lowest fees. You and your colleagues can and should push your employer's human resources department to switch to the most advantageous qualified plan around. Don't accept a plan that isn't optimized to your needs.

Non-Qualified but Tax Advantaged Plans

There are some plans which are technically non-qualified but do provide tax advantages. They may be sponsored by an employer or by you as an individual (i.e., not as an employee). These plans include the Traditional Individual Retirement Account (Traditional IRA) and the Roth IRA. IRAs have lower contribution limits than qualified plans. IRA limits for 2016 are $5,500. If you are over the age of 50, you're allowed a catch-up contribution of $1,000.

While annual contribution limits for IRAs are lower than for 401(k)s, there's usually far greater investment flexibility available in IRAs. You may be able to buy any of thousands of stocks, bonds, mutual funds or exchange traded funds. This makes it easier to diversify your investments, and also gives you the flexibility to select investment funds that have low management fees.

In a Traditional IRA, contributions you make in a given year are made pretax, which means that you can reduce your income tax bill in the year the contribution is made. The investments you make in an IRA grow tax deferred—no taxes until you begin to take money out.

In a Roth IRA, your contributions are made *after* tax. That is, you don't get to lower your taxes in the contribution year. Any gains are tax deferred, but most importantly, *you pay no taxes when you take the money out*. Needless to say, the idea of investing over a long period of time and not having to pay any taxes on gains is very appealing. It's so appealing that everyone wants to do it. But the government limits eligibility for Roth IRAs by income, so in 2016 if you are single and have an adjusted gross income (AGI) of less than $117,000, you can contribute the maximum to a Roth IRA. The permitted contribution gradually phases out, so that once your AGI reaches $132,000, you are likely no longer eligible to contribute to a Roth IRA at all. If you are filing jointly, for 2016 your permitted contribution begins to phase out at a combined AGI of $184,000, and eligibility ends at $194,000.

It's anticipated that the limits for 2017 will remain the same or increase slightly. I suggest you check the IRS website for the latest updates (www.irs.gov).

Non-Qualified and Non-tax Advantaged Accounts

You can also open an investment or brokerage account directly with an investment or brokerage firm. If you choose a *full service* brokerage firm, a broker will be available to recommend purchases or sales of securities such as stocks and bonds, and to implement those trades on your behalf. For each transaction, you pay a commission to the broker.

If you choose a *discount brokerage* firm, the firm will execute your trades, but will not provide you with any advice. Discount brokers, as the name implies, charge lower commissions than full service brokers.

You can also set up an investment account directly with an investment management firm. Examples are Fidelity or Vanguard.

In any of these non-tax advantaged accounts, earnings you receive (in the form of dividends from stocks you own or interest from bonds you own) will be taxable in the year those earnings are received. If you sell any stocks or bonds you may also realize a capital gain (if sold for a profit) or a capital loss (if sold for a loss). In the case of a capital gain, you will be subject to long- or short-term capital gains taxes, depending on whether you held the investment for more or less than a year. Long-term capital gain tax rates are typically lower than short-term gain tax rates.

Keep in mind that from a pure diversification perspective, if you have one of each of these accounts: a 403(b), a Roth IRA, a Traditional IRA, and a discount brokerage account, they may all be investing in similar stocks and bonds (or combinations of stocks and bonds in mutual or exchange traded funds). If that's the case, you may get relatively little diversification benefit across these accounts. You could, of course, purposely hold very different asset classes in each account, carefully selected to make the most of diversification benefits and relative tax advantages. For example, suppose you want to invest 5% of your money in very risky stocks that could yield very high short term capital gains. You could hold small amounts of these risky stocks in each of your accounts, or you may be better off holding these risky securities only in an account that allows tax deferral. This may allow you to avoid being taxed at very high rates on those gains. Municipal bonds are another example. Investors generally don't pay federal taxes on earnings from municipal bonds. Since that tax protection is in place, it makes less sense to hold such securities in tax-advantaged accounts, because there's less benefit to the tax protection.

More generally, since we don't know what future tax legislation may be thrust upon us, there's a basic *tax diversification* argument to be made for holding multiple account types with different tax benefits. Some may be hurt by future legislation, while others may benefit from it.

Some Thoughts on American Stock Market Returns

Many financial planning strategies are based on the assumption that American stock markets will continue to perform as they have over the past century, yielding on average 8% to 10% per year. In accepting these assumptions, advisors and investors are arguably committing the most basic error in the risk management book— they're assuming that the past predicts the future. There's no compelling theory or evidence that guarantees this level of average returns. If anything, one can tell a very different story with far less favorable predictions.

The short version of the story is that after the Second World War every other country in the world that mattered to the global economy had been reduced to rubble. The United Kingdom—ostensibly the military winner in Europe—had been drained over six years of all-out war. The country was on the verge of bankruptcy, and had already or soon would lose many of its colonies. The war effort had been so all-consuming that for several years after the war ended, it was necessary to impose nationwide rationing. The rest of Europe (including France, Italy and other major economies) had been severely mauled by the war. Germany and Russia were devastated. In Asia, similar devastation had been visited upon the Japanese home islands. China, Korea, and other Japanese conquests had also suffered terribly.

Only one country escaped unscathed—the United States of America had not only avoided devastation. It had developed a rich portfolio of new technologies as part of the war effort, in electronics, aviation, machinery, food production, transportation, etc. This meant that the USA had a huge head start on everyone else. Its flexible and bold (albeit imperfect) capitalist system was able to quickly exploit this advantage. The rest of the world had to trade with the USA because for many products, it was the only game in town. Over the next half century this advantage allowed American companies to grow dramatically, giving them a nearly unshakeable global footprint. American companies had unfettered access to just about every market that mattered globally (with the exception of those behind the Iron Curtain). Under such favorable circumstances it's easy to see how American companies and their publicly traded stocks performed very well.

But in comparison to the post war decades, in recent years the American economy has stagnated. Global competition is tougher now than ever before in modern history. China, Brazil, India, and Russia are huge countries with low-wage workforces and increasingly sophisticated engineering and high tech capabilities. Their ability to copy existing products (and increasingly to innovate on their own) makes it possible for them to undermine or undercut American products and services. It doesn't matter whether we view some of these tactics as immoral or underhanded. The point is that there isn't much we can do about them. We also have to compete with all the other industrialized nations—Germany, France, Canada, Australia, Italy, South Korea, among others—and every other developing nation. There's some evidence that we're losing the renewable energy race, ceding leadership, jobs, and prosperity to other countries that have committed to renewable energy faster than us.

Furthermore, our national debt has risen to astronomical levels and our Social Security system is on the verge of insolvency.

Where does all this leave us? It leaves us vulnerable to being wrong as we continue to assume our stock markets will yield 10% annual returns.

I'm not saying all this to cause panic. The bottom line is that we don't know how markets will perform in the next twenty, thirty and forty years. With that recognition, we must fall back on the only logical approach: moderation and diversification. We should consider moderating our assumptions about domestic stock market returns, and we should spread our wealth (diversify) more carefully, across industries and geographies.

Professional Development Timeline

In this chapter I review typical challenges you're likely to face at four stages of professional development: (1) medical, dental, pharmacy, or veterinary student; (2) intern, resident, or fellow; (3) first 'real' job after residency or fellowship; and (4) managerial or ownership role. I make some assumptions regarding *when* certain family obligations or professional risks and opportunities arise. For example, I assume that you're likely to begin a family during the residency/fellowship stage.

I strongly urge you to create a household budget. Appendix 1 contains budgets to match each stage of professional development, using the assumptions alluded to above. Spreadsheet versions of these may be found at www.PillarsOfWealth.com. Feel free to customize these budgets to match your personal circumstances.

Medical/Dental Student

This period (of medical/dental/pharmacy/veterinary studies) is characterized by intense pressures: keeping up with vast volumes of information, not embarrassing yourself in front of peers and professors, and meeting the expectations of family and friends. Responsibilities increase as students begin to have more interactions with patients and their families. And there are the ever-present concerns of realizing how little you know, feeling that everyone else is smarter than you, and fighting off the sense that you are the admissions mistake in your class. As this period comes to an end, you have new concerns: passing board or licensing exams and getting the outcome you want on Match Day. Meanwhile, your debts are steadily piling up.

Medical Student Financial Priorities:

- To the extent possible, avoid student debt. If you must borrow, minimize the use of borrowed funds. Keep in mind that any debt you incur puts you deeper in the hole

- Understand how to manage your growing debts. Get answers to questions such as: How much can you borrow? What are the interest rates? When do you have to begin making payments?

- Know how to contact your lender(s) and how to track the amounts you owe. Make sure you have online access to all relevant records. Be aware of your options: Can you consolidate loans? What are the permissible repayment options?

- Take advantage of grants/fellowships/scholarships whenever possible

- Develop healthy consumption and saving habits

- Live as modestly as you can (without disrupting your studies)

- Consider living with a housemate instead of living alone. This usually means you'll pay less in rent and will be able to share utility costs.

It's difficult during this stage of your career to think about money matters. But making an effort to learn the basics of financial planning will save you time, money, and stress later.

Intern/Resident/Fellow

The internship is characterized by long hours, low pay, exhaustion, and desperate efforts to have a life despite all evidence to the contrary. Student debt burden continues to loom large and may grow even further if you elect to defer payments and capitalize interest payments (raising your loan principal).

The residency is usually similar to the internship, with more exhaustion, more responsibility, and more debt. By this time, you may also have family obligations (spouse and/or children).

The fellowship may be similar to the residency phase in terms of lifestyle (earnings are still quite low) and there's usually even more responsibility and sometimes more debt.

Ironically, the most prestigious hospitals and schools tend to pay their interns, residents, and fellows the smallest amounts. This only makes it harder to make ends meet.

During the internship/residency/fellowship periods your financial concerns tend to be more immediate—for example, the need for money to pay rent and buy groceries. You may have to deposit your meager paycheck quickly just to satisfy outgoing payment obligations. While financial literacy seems more relevant, it often takes a backseat to other priorities—mostly work related. When you do have a minute of time, you prefer to spend it sleeping or doing something social.

Around this time you're likely made aware of the need to obtain insurance and make some investments, but you're overwhelmed by debt and have no disposable income. Insurance may seem like an unnecessary luxury. If all that isn't enough stress, you're worrying about the uncertainty surrounding your first 'real' job search and figuring out that cryptic first employment contract.

Residents/fellows are sometimes told by senior physicians that once they finish graduate studies everything will be fine, because their higher salaries will be sufficient to cover all expenditures. Yes, financial obligations are easier to handle with higher income. But it's not a foregone conclusion that *all* your financial problems will go away. They'll just be different. For example, you'll be required to begin repaying student debt, and you may have new obligations with home and car purchases.

Intern/Resident/Fellow Financial Priorities:

- Live modestly in an effort to make ends meet on your modest salary

- Avoid taking on more debt if possible. Make an informed decision about how to repay existing student loans: can you afford to make some payments? Do you prefer to defer payments? (see the Managing Debt chapter)

- Consider Term life insurance coverage as a cheap way to protect your family (see the Insurance chapter)
- Obtain some basic disability insurance to protect your human capital (see the Insurance chapter)
- If you can afford it, contribute to a 401(k) or 403(b) plan. The key with these plans is to get the full employer match
- If you can afford it, consider contributing to a Roth IRA
- Begin thinking about funding children's college savings plans
- Develop healthy consumption habits—don't over-extend or over-consume—live within your means
- Learn the basics of financial decision making. If your graduate program doesn't offer this, approach your administrators and ask that such education be made available (from an objective source)
- As you near completion of residency/fellowship and are contemplating your first real job offer, seek advice from a qualified attorney regarding your employment contract (see Employment Contract chapter)

The latter point may seem like an unnecessary expense but it's crucial to avoid mistakes at this early stage of your career, when you are least knowledgeable and most vulnerable. Many doctors learn this the hard way. Looking back, they wish they'd consulted an attorney in advance.

Your first contract sets a precedent for all future contracts. Make it a good one!

First 'Real' Job

The good news once you accept your first 'real' job is that for the first time in your career, you should be receiving a much higher salary.

At this career stage you likely want to focus on work and family. You don't want to be distracted by money issues. But you must make good decisions early on to avoid becoming victimized by time value of money errors.

With the expectation of putting down roots and having decent income, many newly employed doctors purchase a first home. This means carrying school debt, a mortgage, and potentially a variety of family obligations (such as day care, babysitting, and school activities). In accounting terms, your balance sheet *explodes* (gets much bigger). In the absence of proper money discipline, even a decent income may not be sufficient to make ends meet.

Upon graduation from your dental, medical, pharmacy, or veterinary program, you have several choices:

- Go directly into your own private practice
- Work as an independent contractor in someone else's practice
- Work as an employee in someone else's private practice
- Work as an employee in a hospital

Here's a joke that's been making the rounds in recent years: *There are two types of doctors: those who work in hospitals and those who want to work in hospitals.* This joke is a reflection of worsening conditions for physicians in private practice. Increasing regulations and cost of malpractice insurance have squeezed private practice earnings, leading many physicians to conclude that the hospital environment is the more stable, safer path. While dentists are subject to some of the same stresses, in general, they have been constrained to a lesser extent than the average physician. Since veterinarians don't treat human patients, they tend to be subjected to less onerous regulation.

A medical or dental practice may insist on hiring you as an independent contractor. This designation is better for the employer, who can avoid some costs. It's better for you to be an employee as opposed to an independent contractor, primarily because you'll be eligible for full benefits.

The IRS scrutinizes independent contractor arrangements, because while the employer may call you an independent contractor, by IRS standards you may, in fact, be eligible to be an employee. The IRS uses several dozen questions to determine the appropriate status. This can lead to some inconvenience in the workplace in the event the IRS ruling conflicts with your employer's interpretation. You can search the IRS site for the latest commentary on this topic.

For those turning to private practice, there's often a contract that sets the terms for buying into a partnership share. Most young physicians and dentists have no idea whether the terms are fair, whether the price is right, and whether it's a good deal. There are sometimes lawyers affiliated with medical and dental programs who can provide advice on the content of such contracts, but it isn't clear that they're giving the best advice. This is why it can be useful to hire your own professional lawyer who specializes in medical or dental contracts. This will help to set you up for success as an attending physician or junior associate in a medical or dental practice.

Attending Physician

The stereotypical attending physician worries about managing his team of fellows/residents/interns, his young family, debt repayment, deciding whether to take a job elsewhere, and trying to distinguish himself from other attending physicians in an effort to increase the probability of promotion. The latter often means seeking a project with which to make an impression on senior faculty. It may be a research initiative, medical management/public health concern, an idea about improving care or decreasing costs, or a more effective way to manage interns/residents.

Junior Associate in Private Medical/Dental Practice

Most dentists go into private practice. They may spend some years in graduate school specializing, but most often post-dental school they take a job as employees in an existing practice.

The typical dentist or physician at this career stage focuses on refining her craft, understanding the business, meeting quotas, being efficient and effective, and doing what is needed to be considered for promotion or a partnership stake.

First Job Financial Priorities:

- Take advantage of 401(k) or 403(b) matching funds by your employer. Your income will likely be too high to qualify for Roth IRA contributions.

- Consider increasing disability insurance coverage to protect your higher income (see Insurance chapter)

- Ensure your life insurance coverage is appropriate (see Insurance chapter)
- Ensure your malpractice insurance is appropriate and in force (it may be covered by your employer)
- Ensure umbrella insurance is appropriate (see Insurance chapter)
- Build a reserve cash fund equivalent to 6 months earnings. This is your rainy day fund
- Your significantly higher earnings mean you are in a higher marginal tax bracket. Consult a qualified accountant to ensure you're taking steps to minimize taxes payable
- Consult an estate planning attorney to draft a Will and related documents. Documents must be state-specific and should be updated as your circumstances and state laws change. (see the Estate Planning chapter)
- Continue to pay back student loans, focusing first on the loans with the highest interest rates
- Diversify across as many pillars of wealth as possible
- Consider purchasing a home and take advantage of tax deductions
- Consider purchasing a rental property
- Set up a college savings plan for your children (as relevant)
- Create a business plan and budget for starting your new practice (if applicable). More guidance on this is provided in the second book in this series: *Pillars of Wealth: Finance and Business Essentials for Medical Practices*
- Don't over-extend or over-consume—live within your means and focus on paying back debt!
- Make financial decisions collaboratively with your partner/spouse. Open communication is crucial to the financial well being and unity of your family.

It may be tempting to splurge with that first of many anticipated large checks. Keep in mind that depreciating assets don't help you to reach your long-term goals. Your financial imperative is to accumulate appreciating assets. This is my unsubtle reminder: *Don't buy the expensive sports car if you have student loans and lots of other obligations.*

You learned to live modestly as a graduate student. If you're carrying student loans, continue living modestly for 3-5 years. This will allow you to generate a lot of excess cash. Use that cash to pay back debt.

If you don't have significant debt, generating excess cash is still a good move which allows you to: save for a down payment on a home, maximize retirement plan contributions, or get a head start on your children's 529 college savings plan.

Managerial/Ownership Role

Regardless of whether you're in private practice or a senior physician in a hospital setting, the main difference compared to your first job is that you now have managerial and/or executive responsibilities. Along with these responsibilities you're enjoying a higher salary.

Managing others, and especially owning your own business, means a new set of challenges and skills. For many, this is not an easy adjustment.

Owner/Partner/Manager Financial Priorities:

- Build your human capital as a manager. Learn how to run a business or hospital division, and how to deal constructively with junior staff members
- Finish paying off school debt
- Diversify across multiple pillars of wealth
- Ensure the rainy day fund is topped-up
- Consider adding more disability insurance coverage as your income rises
- Consider increasing life insurance coverage to protect higher earnings capacity
- Ensure umbrella insurance is at appropriate level

- With your earnings putting you in a high marginal tax bracket, continue to work with a competent accountant

- Work with a competent attorney to ensure estate planning is in place and in particular that your assets are protected. Asset protection looms large now that you have some significant holdings and are aiming to generate even more

- Save. Save. Save. Accumulate appreciating assets. Make the most of your prime earning years!

- Don't over-extend or over-consume—live within your means and save the rest. The more you save, the sooner you can retire.

Periodic Reviews

With each change in your professional (or family) circumstances, you should review your financial situation. These are always good opportunities to take a fresh look at your progress to date and plans for the future.

Get in the habit of making annual reviews. If you elect to work with a financial advisor, she should initiate these annual examinations. If you've decided to do-it-yourself, make time (with your partner if you have one) to ensure your plans are on track.

Managing Debt – Don't Let Your Pillars Sink

One of the toughest challenges faced by medical practitioners is the burden of student loans. Unlike many undergraduate college peers, who get jobs and begin to pay off student loans in their early 20s, those who pursue medical careers incur even greater amounts of debt during medical/dental/pharmacy/veterinary school. And they are often unable to make debt payments as interns, residents and fellows, which can lead to unpaid interest being *capitalized* (added to their outstanding principal).

According to the Association of American Medical Colleges (aamc.org), the median education debt for indebted medical school graduates in 2015 was $183,000. The American Student Dental Association (asdanet.org) states that the average dental student graduate has $241,000 in debt. The main message in these numbers and in numerous articles dealing with the subject is that medical practitioners, weighted down by massive debt burdens, live on a razor's edge.

A *Columbus Dispatch* article puts it this way: "… any financial missteps or career miscalculations can have significant, lifelong consequences." One consequence is that medical practitioners who default on student loans made by the U.S. Department of Health and Human Services may have their licenses revoked or suspended. This, in turn, can disqualify them from participation in programs receiving Medicare and Medicaid reimbursements. Adding insult to injury, a government program dating back to the 1990s set out to publicly shame delinquent medical practitioners by including their names in a Medicare Exclusions List.

Debt burdens go beyond student loans. Real estate lenders tempt doctors with zero (or low) down payment loans. To qualify, a physician or dentist simply has to show an employment letter. Why do lenders do this? Because statistically they know that physicians and dentists exhibit relatively low default rates, and they want to lock them in early as clients. None of these statistics help when you happen to be one of the unfortunate few who runs into financial difficulties.

Some young families face an even greater mountain of debt. I've spoken with several married couples (dual-physician couples; dentist married to physician; physician married to attorney) who have, between them, school debts in excess of $500,000! Add to that more debt for a home mortgage and one or two cars and you've got a very steep challenge.

Now introduce a surprise variable: what if one spouse, clutching that first newborn, decides s/he wants to stay home with the baby? That mountain of debt is suddenly much harder to scale.

The best advice is to live within your means. If you have to borrow, opt for the smallest amount of debt. Instead of the $600,000 palace to compete with your peers, go for the $300,000 starter home. Instead of the sports car, choose something more modest with good gas mileage.

Here's an all-too-common counter example. A doctor calls his accountant and says he needs to talk, urgently. When they meet face to face, the doctor says: *I made around six-hundred thousand dollars last year. This year it looks like I'm only going to make four-hundred thousand.* Then the doctor sighs heavily, and says: *That's not enough, I can't make it on four-hundred thousand. I'm not making enough money. My income is not high enough.*

Mark Rapson, CPA, points out that in most of these cases the problem is not an income issue—*it's a spending issue.* Doctors become accustomed to spending on real estate, cars, private schools, and a variety of other products and services. Some of these expenditures may be justifiable, but objectively, some tend to be unnecessary and inadvisable.

Real Example of Living Within Your Means

Let's turn now to a more encouraging, real life example of good financial decision making. In the early stages of their marriage, Dr. Jones and his wife were on a typical financial trajectory: upon graduation from medical school he had a large amount of school debt, and when they initially settled in Massachusetts, a sizable mortgage. Several years later they found themselves in New Hampshire, with a bigger house, a bigger mortgage, and three children. Around this time Dr. Jones began to question the usual approach of borrowing to fund all major purchases. When it came time to replace the family's two cars, he decided to pay with cash.

This led to a bizarre situation in which the car salesman wasn't sure how to proceed, never before having had to process a car purchase that wasn't financed with debt.

Soon, the family found itself moving to Virginia, and the couple made an explicit decision to avoid debt wherever possible. They bought a house at a price that was well below their purchasing power, allowing them to hold a very small mortgage which was soon paid off. By this time they'd also paid off all school debt.

A decade later, they're still driving the same two cars, two of their children have completed post-secondary education, their daughter is married, and there's enough saved up in a college savings plan for the youngest child to attend college.

The family is now debt-free. Other than replacing the two cars, there are no major expenditures in sight.

The key to being in this favorable position was the family's explicit decision to *live below their means*. This allowed them to pay off debts, ensure high quality education for all (Dr. Jones recently graduated from an Executive MBA program), and put some money away for retirement. Even more impressive is the family's commitment over many years to donate 7-10% of gross income annually to causes such as the Salvation Army, Doctors without Borders, and Mercy Ships.

Repaying Student Loans

Given ongoing congressional debates regarding student loans, please confirm all terms and thresholds through your federal loan representative or private lender before finalizing your borrowing and repayment decisions.

As of mid-2016, 43.3 million Americans have student loans outstanding amounting to $1.26 trillion. Student loan debt is now second only to home mortgage debt in the United States economy. It is larger than car loan debt and all other retail debt types.

According to the Association of American Medical Colleges October 2015 *Debt Fact Card*, the median 4-year Costs of Attendance for graduates of public and private medical schools, respectively, are estimated at $232,838 and $306,171 for the class of 2016.

Some additional observations (Fresne and Youngclaus, 2013):

- There are no discernible gender differences in medical school indebtedness

- Premedical (undergraduate) and non-education debts are a very small portion of outstanding indebtedness by medical school graduates (around $20,000 and $10,000, respectively)

- Grants and scholarships rarely cover the entire cost of medical school, but they are useful in lowering net indebtedness

If you've already completed your education, your focus is on repayment. There are two categories of repayment plans on federal government student loans: *Traditional Repayment* and *Income-Driven*.

Traditional Repayment Plans

Repayment Plan	Terms
Standard Repayment	You have up to 10 years to repay; fixed monthly payments must be at least $50; this plan will cost you the least amount of interest compared to all other plans
Graduated Repayment	You have up to 10 years to repay; initial payments are low and increase every two years; total interest payable by you will be greater than that payable under the Standard Plan
Extended Repayment	You have up to 25 years to repay; choose between graduated payments that increase over time (start low and increase every two years) or fixed payments; monthly payments will be lower than those under Standard Plan, but you'll pay more in interest than Standard Plan

Income-Driven Repayment Plans

Repayment Plan	Terms
Pay As You Earn (PAYE)	You have up to 20 years to repay; if you make the equivalent of 20 years of qualifying payments, any outstanding balance on your loan may be forgiven (you may owe income tax on the forgiven amount); payments will be around 10% of your discretionary income (defined by the Department of Education relative to the poverty line), but never more than you'd pay under the Standard Plan; you'll pay more in interest than under the Standard Plan
Income-Based Repayment (IBR)	You have 20 (or 25) years to repay (depending on whether you had an outstanding balance before July 1, 2014); if you make the equivalent of 20 (or 25) years of qualifying payments, any outstanding balance on your loan may be forgiven (you may owe income tax on the forgiven amount); payments will be around 10% (for new borrowers on or after July 1, 2014) or 15% (for all others) of your discretionary income, but never more than you'd pay under the Standard Plan; you'll pay more in interest than under the Standard Plan
Income-Contingent Repayment (ICR)	You have up to 25 years to repay; payments are the lesser of 20% of your discretionary income, OR, the amount you'd pay on a 12-year Standard Plan multiplied by some income-based percentage; if you make the equivalent of 25 years of qualifying payments, any outstanding balance on your loan may be forgiven (you may owe income tax on the forgiven amount); you'll pay more in interest than under the Standard Plan

Source: https://studentaid.ed.gov/sa/

Federal student loan rules may change over time, so look for the latest updates, which should be available from on-campus sources or from the student aid section of www.ed.gov.

Deferment and Forbearance

Intern, resident and fellow salaries are low. Accordingly, many are unable to make debt payments. This leaves them with one of two options: deferment or forbearance.

Deferment is a period of time during which repayment of your principal and interest is temporarily delayed. In some cases, the federal government may pay the interest on your loans during the deferment period. If you're not eligible for this government subsidy, and you elect not to pay the interest, it may be *capitalized* (added to your loan principal).

If you're unable to make your scheduled loan payments, and you meet certain criteria, your loan servicer may grant you a *forbearance*. This means allowing you to stop making payments or making reduced monthly payments for up to 12 months. Interest will continue to accrue on your subsidized and unsubsidized loans and may be capitalized, thereby increasing your loan principal.

Determine your eligibility for deferment and forbearance at www.studentaid.ed.gov.

Are federal loans a good deal?

For many people, direct lending by the government is the only option available. If parents can't help pay, either from savings, 529 plans, tapping a home equity line of credit, or co-signing a bank loan, federal (or some state) plans may be your only remaining options.

A useful aspect of federal loans is that if you qualify, you *will* get the money. You cannot be refused access to funds if you qualify. Note that graduate PLUS loans are subject to a credit check.

In addition, federal loans are extremely flexible. You can consolidate loans, switch between repayment plans, and survive some delinquency with less damage to your personal credit rating than you would suffer over delinquency on private loans. A private lender would likely declare you in default and refer your case to a collection agency within a matter of months (possibly 90 days). In contrast, federal loan delinquency may extend up to 270 days before you are declared in default.

A default will adversely affect your credit rating, which may haunt you over several years. With federal loans you're allowed an opportunity to make some arranged 'reasonable' payments and rehabilitate your credit record. The government will then inform the credit agencies that you're in good standing, which could allow the default to be expunged from your credit record.

According to the IRS:

> *If your modified adjusted gross income (MAGI) is less than $80,000 ($160,000 if filing a joint return) there is a special deduction allowed for paying interest on a student loan (also known as an education loan) ... This deduction can reduce the amount of your income subject to tax by up to $2,500.*
> – www.irs.gov

A medical resident could get the deduction, but not if she chose the forbearance option in which she opted not to pay during the residency, and instead elected to accrue the interest to principal. You should take this potential deduction into account when deciding which repayment option to use while in residency.

Some other considerations:

- Federal student debt is not dischargeable in bankruptcy. This means the student debt does not go away as a result of bankruptcy filing. You'd still be responsible for paying all that money back. (There can be exceptions in cases where repaying your student loan would cause undue hardship.)

- Loans are dischargeable for total and permanent disability

- When you consolidate federal loans, the resulting interest rate is the weighted average of the individual rates, rounded up to the nearest eighth of a percent

- If you automate loan repayment electronically (auto-debit), you may be able to get a 0.25% (25 basis point) interest rate reduction

- If a borrower works in the public or non-profit sector and pays for 10 years under an Income-Driven or Standard plan, she can have her remaining balance forgiven

In the grand scheme of things, an unsecured loan for which you cannot be rejected, and which gives you access to over $200,000, along with all the flexibility outlined above, can be a decent deal, especially if it's the only source of funds for which you can realistically qualify.

Car Purchase vs. Lease

If you live in an urban area with good public transportation, you may not need a car. This could save you thousands of dollars a year on car payments, gas, parking, repairs, and insurance.

Most of us, however, are highly dependent on our cars, and many households need more than one. As a driver, you have two choices: buy or lease. Unless you're buying with cash (unlikely for most young doctors), you're going to have to make periodic monthly payments under a financing agreement.

The decision to buy vs. lease must make sense within your budget. You can use one of the budget forms from Appendix 1 to estimate how much you can afford monthly for a car. Be sure to include all anticipated costs of ownership of a vehicle in either the purchase or lease scenario. Budget for gas, maintenance, registration, insurance, parking, etc. Gas mileage may be an important consideration in keeping costs low. Also take into account the impact of selecting a used rather than a new vehicle.

Early in your career, I recommend that you avoid making a car into a conspicuous consumption statement. If you must make such a statement, defer it to a much later date, when your household finances are solid.

If you're buying a car, keep the following in mind:

- Do your research ahead of time to identify the fair value of your preferred vehicle. (edmunds.com, invoicedealers.com, (kbb.com, and carsdirect.com may be useful)
- The U.S. Environmental Protection Agency provides information on fuel economy and EPA ratings (fueleconomy.gov)
- Compare dealer financing offers to regular bank loans. The latter may offer better terms
- There's lots of advice available on the web, including when and how to get the best deals, how to negotiate most effectively with dealers, etc.

Consumer Reports and *U.S. News & World Report* are some of the online sources available to address the purchase vs. lease question.

Mortgage Debt

If you decide to purchase a home (or a rental property) you'll most likely take out a mortgage loan. A mortgage loan may be based on fixed or variable interest rates. *Fixed rate* mortgages obligate you to make a constant monthly payment, typically over the course of 30 or 15 years. The monthly payments on *variable rate* mortgages (also known as adjustable rate mortgages or ARMs) are tied to prevailing interest rates, and can be expected to change over time. These mortgage loans often offer low introductory rates for a few years, and then adjust upward (sometimes dramatically). Sometimes you can opt to convert a variable rate loan into a fixed rate loan.

Prior to the Subprime Crisis, many subprime (riskier) loans were variable rate loans. After their initially low introductory rates expired (often after two years), the mortgage payments on these loans rose significantly, forcing many borrowers into default.

Typically, to buy a property you're required to provide a down payment equivalent to 20% of a home's value. You can borrow the remaining 80% in the form of a mortgage loan.

Bankers are well aware that physicians and dentists have high earning capacity and solid creditworthiness. So they love having them as clients. For this reason, you may find banks offering special deals for doctors, including zero down-payment offers. To qualify, you may be required to show prior work experience or some proof of employment such as a copy of your employment contract.

With such seemingly generous terms it can be tempting to buy a large home. But just because you're given the opportunity to buy a home with zero money down, doesn't mean you should take it.

The more of the purchase price you finance through borrowing, the larger your monthly mortgage payments will be. You'll also end up paying more interest over the lifetime of the mortgage.

Furthermore, if your down payment is less than twenty percent of the purchase price, you'll have an extra monthly expense known as Private Mortgage Insurance or PMI.

According to bankrate.com:

> *Private mortgage insurance reimburses the lender if you default on your home loan. You, the borrower, pay the premiums. PMI fees vary, depending on the size of the down payment and your credit score, from around 0.3 percent to about 1.5 percent of the*

original loan amount per year. Some years, PMI premiums are tax-deductible and some years they're not, depending upon the whim of Congress.

Buying vs. Renting

Historically, government policies and popular American culture encouraged home ownership, while portraying renting as 'throwing money away.' In the wake of the Subprime Crisis many people have revised their thinking about homeownership.

Some benefits of home ownership were discussed in the earlier Pillars of Wealth chapter. These included the appeal of owning a tangible, physical asset you can see and touch, the long-term record of real estate as an appreciating asset—one that does reasonably well in inflationary periods, and potential tax deductions.

It's easy to get caught up in home ownership euphoria. Yes, real estate investments have many positives, but you must be aware of the full picture before diving in.

First, you must decide whether you can *afford* to purchase a home:

- Can you qualify for a mortgage? Is your credit history sufficiently solid?

- Can you afford the monthly payments? What are the levels of current interest rates and what are they expected to be in future? Very high rates make it difficult to meet monthly payment obligations

- Do you qualify for a decent fixed rate mortgage, which takes interest rate risk out of the picture? In contrast, an adjustable rate mortgage means that if interest rates rise, your monthly payments may rise dramatically

Next, you have to be sure you *want* to own a home. Here are some potential drawbacks to owning your own home:

- If you elect to own your home and purchase it with a mortgage, you're committing to a long period of fixed monthly obligations. If your income declines, for whatever reason, paying that fixed amount each month becomes harder

- As an owner you must pay to maintain the home. Expect a steady stream of payments for various maintenance projects, including, among others: roofing repairs, landscaping, driveway resurfacing, updating a kitchen and bathrooms, etc.

- Do you want to deal with the added administrative costs of owning a home (property taxes, insurance, lawn care, trash removal, Home Owners Association dues, condominium fees, electric or other utilities, etc.)? Can you afford these costs? Newer homes tend to have lower maintenance costs but higher property taxes

- Property taxes can be significant, especially for a new property in an expensive neighborhood

- As noted in the Cash Pillar segment, real estate is an illiquid asset. This means that money invested in real estate is locked up for a long period

- While real estate has proven to be a fairly reliable investment over long periods of time, significant value declines can occur. We experienced that as a result of the Subprime Crisis. A long-term investor can ride out such volatile periods, but owners who have to sell during market declines may face deep losses

As a renter, you can avoid these downsides, but must give up the homeownership benefits. There's nothing wrong with electing to rent a home rather than purchasing. Giving yourself an extra year or two to save up for a down payment and make sure you pick the correct neighborhood can be an astute move. Renting also means avoiding a mountain of debt. In hindsight, clearly more people should have opted to rent in the mid-2000s. Instead, millions of people took on unaffordable debt and lost their homes.

There are several calculators that can help you make the buy vs. rent decision. One example is BankRate.com. A URL is included in the Resources section of this book.

As a rule of thumb, if you're going to be living in a particular location for less than four years, you would most likely be better off renting rather than buying. This is primarily because of various fees and closing costs that you must pay to purchase a home.

According to Zillow.com:

> *Typically, home buyers will pay between about 2 to 5 percent of the purchase price of their home in closing fees. So, if your home*

cost $150,000, you might pay between $3,000 and $7,500 in
closing costs. On average, buyers pay roughly $3,700 in closing
fees, according to a recent survey.

By law lenders must provide closing cost estimates to you within three days of receiving your loan application.

The lender may offer to waive some closing costs. But beware, sometimes the lender will make up for this concession by charging you a higher rate of interest, which can add up to much more over 30 years of mortgage payments.

Home Equity Line of Credit (HELOC)

A feature of property ownership is that you may be able to borrow money against the equity value in your home using a home equity line of credit, also known as a HELOC. A HELOC helps to mitigate real estate illiquidity by giving you access to cash. But you must set up the HELOC in advance so that it's properly approved and ready to go when the need arises.

Setting up the line of credit may take a few weeks, but once set up, you can get the funds on very short notice. Usually, you'll have checks or a credit card connected to the account. Any funds you withdraw will then require you to pay interest. When you pay off the loan your account once again goes into undrawn status. Usually, you pay a relatively small annual fee to keep the line of credit open.

In some cases your bank may offer to waive some of the costs of setting up a line of credit.

But! And this is a big but, just because the bank is willing to give you a HELOC doesn't mean you should get one. The collateral for the HELOC is your home. Failure to pay back the interest or principal could result in the lender foreclosing on your home. As always, you must think very carefully before taking on any credit obligations.

No one goes into debt assuming they'll miss payments. But it does happen. What are some implications of missing a mortgage payment?

Implications of Missing a Mortgage Payment

Missing even a single mortgage payment is bad, because it could be setting you on a path to losing your home and all the money you've put into it. If you appear to be on the verge of missing a payment, let your lender know immediately. The lender can usually make arrangements for you to make up a month's rent later instead of initiating proceedings that will hurt your credit rating.

But don't miss another payment! Lenders may work with you once, but multiple occurrences will not be met with much sympathy. Because you don't ever want to be in this situation, you must budget properly before purchasing a home. Make sure you're aware of all the costs of acquiring a home and that you're certain you can afford the monthly payments. The best way to do this is to create and maintain a household budget. (See Appendix 1 for some samples).

Credit Cards

Credit cards are often the silent killer. It's extremely tempting to buy things using a plastic card. It doesn't seem like real money, and you can have anything you want ... until the bills begin to roll in.

Credit card companies allow you to make small minimum monthly payments to support a large balance. That may seem convenient initially, but the interest rates on ongoing balances can be in excess of 20% annually! This is a deadly rate. Generally, you're far better off seeking a loan from a bank than borrowing using a credit card.

The safest solution is not to rely on a credit card as a borrowing source. Instead view it as a convenience—avoiding the need to carry cash—and pay off all monthly balances in full. Don't use credit cards to pay for anything that will require an ongoing monthly balance. (Zero-interest financing may be an exception—as long as you don't miss any payments that trigger high interest rates). If you can't easily pay off your monthly balance, whatever purchase you're considering is unaffordable, and represents living beyond your means.

Another alternative is to view credit cards as a way to accrue frequent flyer miles. But that's it! Always pay off your balance in full.

Of course, the most dependable way to avoid credit card debt is very simple—don't carry credit cards with you. Keep yourself on a strict cash diet. That may seem over the top in a modern economy where everything works on magnetized plastic cards. *And who has time to go to the bank to withdraw cash?* But if you don't have a credit card, you can't have credit card debt. So if you know you have a predilection for abusing the privilege of owning a card—cut it up! And if you must participate in the modern electronic economy, get a debit card. Debit cards don't extend you a loan (with murderous interest rates). They simply tap into your existing bank balance.

If you really can't make ends meet, you're back to seeking a loan from the bank; one that will be manageable. In stating this I'm assuming you're a student who must resort to borrowing due to high education-related costs. If you've completed your undergraduate and graduate medical education and you are gainfully employed, it's difficult to accept the necessity for more loans. More likely, you must take an honest look at your budget and cut out unnecessary expenses. If your income isn't going up, your expenditures must come down. The math is simple.

Your Credit Score

Credit scores are generated using statistical models and are used to assess your *creditworthiness*. That is, how likely or unlikely you are to pay your bills. For example, banks, car dealerships, and insurers are all likely to request your credit report and credit scores when deciding whether to provide you with products or services. Even prospective employers like to use credit scores as a proxy for candidates' sense of financial responsibility.

Credit scores are generated using credit report information. In the United States, such information typically comes from the three major credit bureaus: Equifax, Experian, and TransUnion.

A credit report compiles all available data on your payment history from banks, credit card companies, collection agencies, governments, etc. Your credit score results from applying a statistical model to the information in your credit report, along with any other relevant information that may help to predict delinquency.

Over the years the models used to generate credit scores have increased in sophistication. But that does not mean such scores are perfect predictors of a borrower's creditworthiness. Furthermore, many consumers complain that their underlying reports contain errors.

As a consumer you're entitled to see your credit report every 12 months from each of the major bureaus. Note this applies to the credit *reports*, not the credit *scores*. You can purchase your credit scores from the bureaus. There may be other opportunities to see your scores. For example, you may be entitled to see them as part of a loan application process.

A low credit score can dramatically raise your borrowing costs. It may even lead to denial of your credit application (for a home, car, or insurance purchase). So you should periodically request free copies of your reports to ensure they're accurate. There's a formal mechanism for disputing the contents of your reports.

If your score is low, you should take immediate action to rehabilitate it. The process can take years, so you must begin as soon as possible.

Your bank, the credit bureaus, and many other resources can provide you with advice on how to improve your credit score. One such resource is provided in the Resources section of this book (see FICO). You may also wish to consider meeting with a credit counselor.

Managing Risk – Anticipating Threats to Your Pillars

I consider this to be one of the most important chapters in this book. This is primarily because the concept of risk is so important, and yet is often misunderstood. Unfortunately, it's often misunderstood by providers of financial advice. Relatively few financial professionals truly understand the probabilistic nature of risk. Instead, they tend to parrot one-liners they learned while preparing for licensing exams or during sales training sessions.

In this chapter we define risk and return, discuss how each is measured, and how the two can be combined in the form of risk-return ratios to empower financial decision making.

Risk and Reward

Financial decisions ultimately boil down to two simultaneous considerations:

1. How much *risk* is involved, and
2. How much *reward* (or return) is expected

Doctors understand the interplay between risk and reward. There are often multiple treatment options for a given patient (usually one of those choices is to do nothing). Each choice is accompanied by some amount of risk, and some potential gain in terms of improved health. The key is to form a judgment about which choice yields the superior tradeoff.

More generally, decisions in any setting (medical, financial, political, etc.) must *simultaneously* take into account both risk and return. This is a crucial observation. Sellers of financial products and services invariably try to get you to focus on one or the other. They will try to tempt you (the 'greed' motive) by focusing on rewards or returns, or they will try to scare you by focusing on risk (the 'fear' motive). You must always insist on considering both together, in balanced fashion.

Thus, the golden rule of financial decision making is: *Always make decisions based on simultaneous and objective consideration of risk and return!*

What is Risk?

Risk arises when we engage in activities that yield uncertain outcomes with potentially negative consequences.

Consider rolling a pair of dice, or tossing a coin. You're *uncertain* about which numbers between one and six the dice will settle on, or whether the coin will land on 'heads' or 'tails.' When at least one outcome has negative consequences, you face *risk*. For example, if you bet money on the dice roll or coin toss outcome, you are facing risk. On the other hand, if there's no money at stake—that is, no downside—we would say the situation is uncertain, but not strictly speaking risky.

Generally, a negative outcome may come in the form of potential financial loss, property destruction, physical injury, reputational damage, emotional setback, etc.

Some risky scenarios such as the dice roll or coin toss may exhibit only a handful of distinct potential outcomes {1, 2, 3, 4, 5, 6} or {heads, tails}. When you invest in the stock market there are potentially many negative outcomes. These cover a wide spectrum of small to very large losses. When you start your own private practice, you face various risks, with a wide range of potential outcomes spanning low positive earnings to negative earnings to outright bankruptcy.

As a medical professional you understand the concept of risk. You know that a disease or injury may lead to pain or death. You also know that any treatment regimen introduces potential undesirable consequences including secondary infections or other complications.

Likelihood and Severity

Risk is often divided into two dimensions:

1. The *probability* or *likelihood* of a negative outcome occurring, and
2. The *severity* of damage in the event a negative outcome occurs

For example, a bank considers lending money to a medical practice. The first dimension of risk the bank faces is the possibility that the borrowing practice will go bankrupt (this is the probability of the negative outcome). The second dimension is the amount of the loan that may be lost due to the bankruptcy (this is the severity of the negative outcome).

To mitigate the first dimension (the probability of default) the bank will closely examine the medical practice's proposed business plan, its intended location, the experience and credibility of its management team, etc. To mitigate the second dimension (the size of the loss) the bank will demand collateral: including specific assets to secure the loan, such as real estate, equipment, inventory, etc.

It's easy to get caught up in discussions of negative outcomes. But most of us don't take risks for the sake of risk. We take risks because we expect some reward or return.

What is Return?

Return refers to the upside or benefit we seek from participating in some activity. The return or reward may be physical, emotional, or financial. In our financial context the risky activity is investing.

Investment returns come in several forms:

1. *Income* we receive on investments (dividends received on stocks, interest received on bonds, or rent payments on property we own), and
2. *Capital gains* from selling assets (stocks, real estate, a medical practice) at prices that are higher than what we paid for them

Consistently generating positive returns on investments helps to steadily grow our pillars of wealth.

Risk Tolerance, Risk Aversion, Risk Appetite

As noted earlier, the golden rule of financial decision making is: *Always make decisions based on simultaneous and objective consideration of risk and return.*

The golden rule leads to some fundamental questions: *Can we be objective about risk? Do we all feel the same way about risk?*

Not surprisingly, it turns out that we all have different tolerances or appetites for risk, and we may feel very differently about the same risk. Most of us are somewhat conservative and don't like facing risk at all. We have a low appetite for risk or a low tolerance for risk. We're happy taking little to no risk, in return for a modest return. Economists would describe us as 'risk averse.'

In contrast, a smaller percentage of the population falls under the category of gamblers or *risk lovers*. Risk lovers have a large capacity to tolerate risk or a big appetite for risk. These are the people who go bungee diving, jump out of planes, and generally tempt fate. Their reward for these daredevil activities seems to be the adrenalin rush, and they find that sufficient.

Because people have different attitudes toward risk (some of us are more averse to risk than others, and some of us love risk to varying degrees), we don't all react the same way to the same risky situation.

Let's set up an experiment to distinguish people's relative levels of risk aversion. Begin by arranging a scenario with a fixed level of risk, and then measuring how much reward (for example, how much money) must be promised to each person to get them to agree to take that risk. The most risk-averse among us will require the highest reward to accept the risk, whereas the risk lovers will accept the risk just for the thrill of it, with little to no financial reward. The reward each person demands in order to accept the risk can be called that person's *risk premium*. We can sort the people by risk premium, from highest to lowest. This yields a ranking by risk preference. The people at the top of the list are the most risk averse, and hence require the highest risk premium to accept the risky deal. At the bottom of the list are the risk lovers.

Government regulators (and common sense) require brokers and financial advisors to understand each client's risk tolerance. This is meant to ensure clients receive products that match their risk preferences.

A highly risk averse investor should end up with a very conservative (low risk) portfolio and only a person with low risk aversion (high tolerance for risk) should be allowed to enter into very risky investments.

Measuring Risk Tolerance

The concept of risk aversion is perfectly sensible in theory: If we can measure risk tolerance we should do so. The problems begin when we attempt to do this in practice. The most common method used to measure risk aversion is a questionnaire. But it's not always easy for investors to answer the questions accurately. It's not that they don't want to. It's because the wording of questions may bias the answers, or because investors aren't sufficiently in tune with their feelings about risk to provide accurate answers.

In fact, investors are likely to answer the same questions differently depending on their state of mind, which may be highly influenced by external conditions. For example, an investor may feel extremely vulnerable immediately following a market crash, leading to conservative answers to the questionnaire (*once bitten, twice shy*). That same investor, six months earlier, during the giddiest moments of a spectacular boom market, may well exhibit overconfidence, giving answers consistent with a very high tolerance for risk.

Here are some typical questionnaire entries:

1. Which would you prefer to invest in?
   (a) Highly diversified portfolios
   (b) Individual company stock
   (c) A single startup company

Here, the answer (a) suggests high risk aversion, while (c) suggests low aversion to risk.

Another potential question might be:

2. If the stock market declined by 20% tomorrow, would you:
   (a) Sell all your stock investments?
   (b) Sell half of your stock investments?
   (c) Buy more stock?

In this example, a highly risk averse investor would be expected to choose (a), while a risk loving investor might choose (c).

On the surface, these questions appear to reveal risk aversion. But as already noted, our risk aversion changes over time and is affected by circumstances. The upshot is that we cannot always answer such questions objectively. For example, when asked these questions in the midst of a decade-long boom market, I may totally forget the anxiety associated with a 20% market decline. This may lead me to believe (since such a decline is now unthinkable for me) that the aggressive choices are the most favorable. But in reality, my natural risk aversion is high, and when markets actually decline precipitously I would be so overcome by fear and anxiety that I would lose sleep and desperately wish I'd selected the conservative choices.

The real point here is that there's a *Catch-22*. The only way I can accurately answer questions designed to reveal my risk tolerance is if I already know my risk tolerance. Many people don't understand enough about the emotional context of decision making to answer these questions objectively. Unsophisticated financial advisors are also susceptible to this. For them providing the questionnaire is equivalent to checking a box for the purposes of compliance and legal liability coverage. They don't understand the limitations of the process from a risk tolerance identification perspective.

If you want to sleep well at night, you must carefully consider your comfort level with risk. Try to imagine how you (and your partner) would feel under various market downturns. Then ask yourself: *Are my (our) current circumstances (for example: investment choices and insurance coverage) consistent with my (our) feelings about risk?*

Remember, your evaluation of risk preferences should take into account how you will feel when things go wrong!

There are analogies to these concepts in other aspects of our lives. For example, we may enter our first romantic relationship without any regard to the potential downsides (very low risk aversion). But by the next relationship we're likely to be more guarded—more reluctant to commit fully to what we know is an emotionally vulnerable scenario.

Those of us who have had a really bad relationship, especially when the memories are fresh, tend to be very reluctant to take the plunge again (we are extra risk-averse). We'd have to see a really large benefit or reward before working up the courage to plunge back into dating or loving. We often see this theme in books and movies: the hero or heroine, coming off a bad relationship, is reluctant to begin another one (fear of high severity outcome), but is inspired to commit upon fatefully encountering a soul mate (high reward).

Measuring Return

As noted earlier, returns come in two forms: income (from dividends, interest, and rental sources), and capital gains.

When measuring returns, we must distinguish between realized and expected returns: *Realized* (or historical) returns are those that have already happened. That is, we received dividends or interest or capital gains. *Expected* (or future) returns are those that have yet to manifest. Think of these as paper gains; we're anticipating some gains, but have not yet received them.

Realized Return

To measure *realized* return we need three items:

1. How much we paid for the original investment (the *Purchase price*)
2. How much we received when we sold it (the *Sale price*), and
3. Any Cash we received (or paid) while owning the asset. Cash received includes interest or dividend payments

The Purchase and Sale prices determine the capital gains component of returns. The realized return is given by a simple formula:

$$\text{Realized Return} = \frac{\text{Sale Price} - \text{Purchase Price} + \text{Cash Received} - \text{Cash Paid}}{\text{Purchase Price}}$$

This measure is also known as the *Holding Period Return*. It's the return we receive over the period during which we held or owned the asset. *Cash Received* refers to any payments received from the investment (cash inflows) during the period; for example, dividends or interest income. *Cash Paid* refers to any payments needed to sustain the investment (cash outflows). For example, maintenance costs on real estate investment.

Say we bought a single share of a company's equity at $10. A year later we receive a dividend of $2, and immediately after that we sell the stock for $14. Then our realized return is:

$$\text{Realized Return} = \frac{\$14-\$10+\$2}{\$10} = 60\%$$

If no dividend is received, the holding period return is simply the percentage change in price, or the *Capital Gain*:

$$\text{Realized Return} = \text{Capital Gain only} = \frac{\$14-\$10}{\$10} = 40\%$$

If the Sale Price is lower than our Purchase Price, we realize a Capital Loss.

Of course, before popping champagne bottles to celebrate favorable returns, we first have to make some payments.

These include:

- Fees or commissions for buying or selling financial securities
- Fees to financial advisors for managing our money
- Taxes to various government entities (federal, state, etc.).

Taxes are usually payable if we've made money. If we lose money, we can sometimes get tax benefits. Consult with your accountant to ensure you're making the most of these potential tax reductions.

All costs must be subtracted from the original return measures to obtain net returns, which are the amounts of money that actually make it into our pockets.

Expected Return

The general format of expected return calculation is similar to that of realized return. We generally need three items:

1. The Purchase price
2. The Sale price, and
3. Any Cash or Income received (or paid)

The challenge with *expected* return calculations is that we don't know the Sale Price—because the sale has not yet taken place.

We also don't know whether we will receive any income (e.g., interest or dividends). We may have been *promised* such payments, but there's a possibility the other party won't pay up.

Let's use a real estate example to calculate expected return. You're thinking of buying a home currently priced at $180,000. Your intention is to sell it in five years. You want to estimate the expected return on the investment. You don't know what the final (sale) price will be (this is the source of uncertainty or risk), so you need an extra step before applying the holding period return formula.

Relying on locally sourced data, you come up with a simple model. It assumes that in five years one of three outcomes may come about:

1. The first outcome assumes the economy will be strong, with the property rising in value to $315,000
2. The second outcome assumes a slow but steady economic expansion, with the property rising to $200,000
3. The third outcome assumes economic contraction, leading to a decline in the property value to $160,000

Finally, you assume that the three outcomes are equally likely. That is, each outcome occurs with a probability of one third ($\frac{1}{3}$).

The expected (average) value of the property at the end of the fifth year is:

$$\text{Expected Value} = \frac{\$315,000 + \$200,000 + \$160,000}{3} = \$225,000$$

Now we can apply the holding period return formula, using this expected value as the final property value or Sale Price. This yields an expected return of:

$$\text{Expected Return} = \frac{\$225,000 - \$180,000}{\$180,000} = \$45,000 \text{ or } 25\%$$

Alternatively, you could calculate the return under each scenario, and then form an expectation (weighted average) of those returns across all scenarios. This is shown in the table, below.

Economic Scenario	Asset's Sale Price	Return
Strong	$315,000	$\frac{\$315,000 - \$180,000}{\$180,000} = 75\%$
Steady Expansion	$200,000	$\frac{\$200,000 - \$180,000}{\$180,000} = 11.1\%$
Contraction	$160,000	$\frac{\$160,000 - \$180,000}{\$180,000} = -11.1\%$
Average Return $= \frac{75\% + 11.1\% - 11.1\%}{3} = 25\%$		

To obtain a more accurate return measure we'd need to account for other cash flows. For example, we ignored broker fees, taxes, and maintenance costs on the property. We also assumed this would be a primary home. For a rental property we'd expect to receive rental income. We'd likely want to perform more detailed calculations on a monthly or annual basis.

Measuring Risk

Twenty-thousand years ago risk was well understood.

It usually came in the form of a nasty predator that was: larger than us, faster than us, or had bigger teeth than us. We didn't need to quantify the risks—we just needed to run from them.

In the modern world we deal with a multitude of complex risks. The intuition we've evolved over millions of years to handle the natural world often doesn't apply well to modern risks (the concepts of evolutionary psychology and psychological barriers to decision making are explored in the next chapter).

In response we've developed quantitative measures meant to address modern risks. Two risk measures designed for the investing context are *volatility* and *covariance*.

Volatility (Total Risk)

Volatility is a measure of how much variability there is in uncertain outcomes. Technically, the volatility measures dispersion around a mean. It's simply the square root of the variance of observed historical outcomes (e.g., returns on a stock or a bond). It's often assumed that this historical variability will continue in future, so the historical volatility measure becomes our expectation of future volatility (This in itself is a shaky assumption but we'll ignore it for now).

Let's apply the calculation to returns on a stock. First, compile a list of 60 sequential monthly return observations for our stock. Next, calculate the average of the historical returns. Now subtract the average return from each historical return and square the differences. Add all the differences up and divide this sum by the number of return observations (60). This quantity is the variance. Its square root is the volatility, popularly labeled as the Greek letter sigma (σ).

Volatility (σ) quantifies the likelihood of obtaining unfavorable returns (those that are far below the mean). Since σ captures all the economic, political, and other factors that drove the stock's returns (over the period of interest—60 months), this quantity is known as the measure of *total risk*. A large σ suggests high dispersion in the underlying distribution of returns (both in the past and future), and therefore higher likelihood or probability of a really bad (low or negative return) outcome.

Covariance (Systematic Risk)

To understand the covariance measure we need to recognize that total risk can be decomposed into two components: *diversifiable* and *non-diversifiable* risk (the latter is often also referred to as *systematic* risk).

The covariance measure takes center stage when we assert a financial principle which says that financial markets don't reward investors for taking total risk. They reward only systematic risk exposure. The assumption is that any diversifiable risk can and should be diversified, leaving only the systematic or non-diversifiable risk. If we accept this principle, then we need a measure of that systematic risk or exposure. That measure is known as beta (β).

Systematic risk is the risk that all investments are subjected to because they exist in the same market, or economy (or system). Sources of systematic risk include the prices of oil and other strategic commodities, market-wide interest rates, and general economic growth rates. Non-systematic sources of risk are those that are investment specific. For example, when I invest in a particular stock, I understand that the stock price (and hence my returns) may decline if the CEO of the firm becomes ill, or if a major client of the firm decides to cancel a big contract.

The *system* is by definition the entire market. So when we talk about a security's systematic risk we are really trying to estimate how its returns move with respect to the system or market as a whole. In other words, we are interested in the covariance between the two. An investment (e.g., a stock) that has a very large β exhibits price movements (and hence returns) that move more wildly than the market. Low β investments have returns that move less dramatically than the market.

The standard way to calculate β for a given investment is to compile historical returns for the security (stock) in question, and line those returns up against the total Market returns over the exact same period. The Market in this context is an almost mythical concept that encompasses all traded assets in an entire economy. Since there is no such measure, a proxy is used. In the USA that proxy is often the S&P 500 index—a portfolio of 500 large American corporations. We can use data over three, five, or ten years, or whatever we feel is appropriate. We first subtract the risk free rate from both series of returns (the stock in question and the Market). This yields quantities known as *excess returns* for both our stock and the Market. Finally, we regress the excess returns of the security in question on the excess returns of the Market over the comparable period. The slope coefficient of that regression is our estimate of β. Mathematically, β embodies the covariance between the security returns and the Market returns. By definition, the β of the Market (regressing Market returns on Market returns) is equal to exactly 1.

Relying on Others for Risk Assessments

Because financial markets are so complex, measuring risk on our own is often impractical. So, instead, we rely on measures of risk produced by others. Examples are: σ and β estimates produced by analysts, and bond ratings from credit rating agencies such as Moody's and Standard & Poor's.

Hopefully you recognize that risk is a probabilistic concept—there are multiple potential outcomes, each of which has some probability of occurring.

The commonly used risk measures we've discussed all seek to summarize risk with a single number or label. For example, $\sigma=14.8\%$, $\beta=1.2$, or rating=AA. Such efforts are doomed to fail, because *no single number or label can reflect an entire distribution of outcomes*. Nevertheless, the majority of professional financial market participants continue to rely on these simplistic measures.

The risk measurements we discussed above are flawed. But that doesn't mean they're useless. The key is to consider their inherent weaknesses before using them to make decisions. The flaws are examined more closely in an *Investments & Wealth Monitor* article: "Understanding Uncertainty and Common Risk Management Challenges."

Financial Advisors Rarely Understand Risk's Nuances

Each of the risk measures mentioned above has serious flaws. But all continue to be widely calculated, used, and abused by financial advisors, agents, and brokers.

Why is that?

The answer is that these measures proliferate because they're easy to calculate. When it comes to measuring risk in financial markets, 'easy' is often a winning argument. As disappointing as this seems, it underlies a disturbing truth: Many finance professionals don't really understand risk and risk measures.

They memorize a few catchy phrases from their licensing exam preps and parrot them for the remainder of their careers. Keeping things simple allows them to steer/control clients.

I can usually tell whether an advisor is worthy of further consideration within five minutes of conversation. I purposely move the discussion to the subject of risk and wait for the advisor to prove his ignorance. Sadly, it usually doesn't take very long.

Risk-Return Ratios

Let's revisit the golden rule: financial decisions should only be taken after considering the simultaneous interplay of risk and expected return.

We can create measures that include both elements in the form of *risk-return* ratios.

Two ratios we could use for decision making are:

1. *Sharpe Ratio* or *reward-to-volatility ratio*, which is the Excess Return divided by σ, and
2. *Treynor Ratio*, the Excess Return divided by β

The Sharpe ratio is the excess return per unit of total risk, and the Treynor ratio is the excess return per unit of systematic risk. Excess return is the expected return minus the risk-free rate of return.

We can calculate these ratios (and there are other measures as well) and use them to evaluate the risk-return tradeoffs offered by various securities. We favor securities with larger ratio values, which indicate a higher expected return per unit of risk taken.

Generally, we should use volatility (σ) and Sharpe Ratio when comparing stand alone investments. For example, if I have a choice between two large portfolios and I don't care how they relate to any of my other financial holdings, I would select the portfolio with the higher Sharpe Ratio.

In contrast, say I own a diversified portfolio and now I'm considering adding another investment to that portfolio. Here I need to take into account how an additional investment will relate to my existing portfolio (I need to consider the covariance between the two). In such cases I'd seek an investment with a relatively high Treynor Ratio. A high Treynor Ratio suggests an investment with relatively high expected return given its β. Another way to say that is that the investment has relatively low systematic risk. Adding an investment with low systematic risk means that my overall portfolio's risk will be diversified even further. This will improve my existing portfolio's risk-return characteristics.

Is Risk Good or Bad?

Inherently, risk is neither good nor bad. Labels such as good or bad apply when we are assessing *risk-taking behavior*, in which we examine whether a person is logically assessing both the risk and expected return of a proposed decision. In this context, rather than using the labels good and bad, it's more helpful to think in terms of constructive versus destructive risk-taking behavior.

Constructive Risk-Taking

Risk-taking can be extremely beneficial to individuals and societies. For example, entrepreneurial risk-taking can pay off in innovation and progress. Even when a specific outcome is not achieved, we learn and make progress by taking chances: many of the best lessons are the ones learned the hard way—by trying and failing.

Our society was formed and advanced by risk-takers. Ceasing to take risks would bring to a halt everything our society depends on. It would end experimentation, innovation, renewal, challenge, excitement, and motivation.

While there are individuals and even societies that shun risk-taking, most cultures revere risk-taking. This is exemplified in the motto embraced by many elite fighting units: *who dares wins.*

Destructive Risk-Taking

In some cases, risk taking is completely out of proportion to any expected rewards, and only exposes people to danger. Some destructive risk-taking examples include compulsive gambling, driving while intoxicated, and engaging in unsafe sexual activity. Such risky behavior may be rooted in psychological problems, and may reflect a cry for help, warranting attention.

It's not always clear whether an individual is engaging in constructive or destructive risk-taking. Often, this only becomes clear with the benefit of hindsight. Many important human achievements were originally viewed as destructive by mainstream society, and the poor souls who took anti-establishment risks were often ostracized—or worse. Italian astronomer, physicist, engineer, philosopher, and mathematician Galileo Galilei exemplified this by publicly stating that the earth revolved around the sun. At the time this was viewed as heretical in a society that believed god made the earth the center of the universe. Galileo was tortured by the authorities. His courage inspired the pursuit of truth through science.

Here's an example of risk taking in the medical context: Centuries ago, cutting into cadavers in order to learn about human anatomy was illegal and occasionally viewed as witchcraft. Physicians had to take risks to learn about the inner workings of the human body. They often had to pay shady characters to exhume recently buried corpses which could then be secretly examined. Those who took such risks were able to gain practical knowledge that was unavailable to others, making them better physicians. Of course, while we can now view such efforts as constructive, authorities at the time viewed them as criminal.

Opportunity Cost

One of the greatest mistakes people commit when making decisions is forgetting to take into account the cost of *not* selecting particular alternatives. A decision not to pursue a risky goal can mean depriving oneself of a significant windfall. More meaningfully, it may deprive society of important progress. This lost windfall is known as the *opportunity cost* of the decision. That is, the cost of turning down an opportunity.

Suppose I am facing two choices:

1. Working as a physician in a hospital
2. Going into private practice

The opportunity cost of selecting (1) is giving up the additional income that may be available in private practice and the flexibility of running my own business. The opportunity cost of selecting (2) is foregoing the peace of mind of having a steady job and not having to spend a lot of time and effort on management of a private practice.

Risk Handling Alternatives

We have four choices when faced with a risk: we can: retain, avoid, transfer, or reduce it. These risk-mitigation alternatives are discussed below.

Retention or Acceptance

Retention of risk refers to accepting the risk as is, without taking any action to reduce or avoid it. In a medical setting, this is equivalent to saying, *I know I face the risk of a malpractice suit, but I don't care. I'm just going to keep doing what I'm doing, and I'm not getting malpractice insurance.*

Other examples include going for a walk in the dark without an escort or not paying for flood or earthquake insurance.

Avoidance

Avoidance refers to not taking on the risk in the first place. In our example, it's like saying, *I can't stand the idea of facing the risk of a malpractice suit, so I'm either not going to be a physician/dentist, or I'm not going to perform procedures that expose me to lawsuits.*

In a general risk management context, this is equivalent to setting the first dimension of risk—the probability of the bad outcome—to zero. I.e., *if I don't participate, the bad event can't happen.*

Other examples include not buying a stock, not making a financial investment, not going mountain climbing or whitewater rafting, or not going into private practice.

Transfer

Transfer refers to giving the risk to another party, as in, *I don't want to be devastated by a malpractice suit, so I'm paying an insurance company to take on that financial risk instead of me. I'm passing that risk on to someone else.*

Paying an insurance company doesn't address the first dimension of risk. We're not reducing the probability of the bad outcome. Instead, we're contracting another party (the insurer) to take care of the second dimension of the risk for us. Our severity goes to zero (in reality, the severity is limited to our deductible) because the insurer is footing the big bill.

Of course, the insurer will try to get us to alter our behavior in order to reduce the probability of the bad outcome. The insurer will contractually obligate us to use proper procedures and supplies, along with any other requirements it can impose that reduce its risk exposure.

Reduction

Reduction refers to taking some actions that lower the risk exposure. To minimize medical lawsuit exposure, you can ensure a sterile work environment, hire only highly qualified and careful professionals, and ensure compliance with all regulatory requirements. This addresses both dimensions of risk: by being careful in the workplace you reduce the probability of injury that leads to a lawsuit. Being conscientious in delivering your services can reduce the severity of a damages award. You would likely face a more punitive award if it could be shown that your practice was not compliant with regulations, or had acted negligently.

Other reduction examples include taking positions in financial derivatives that hedge some investing risk, buying disability insurance coverage to replicate part of your income, or embracing healthier eating habits to lower the likelihood of obesity or vascular disease.

Ultimately, selection among these four actions depends on the expected return on each risk, the cost of the risk-mitigating action, and your risk tolerance.

Financial Decision Making

You made it this far in your career because you're able to make professional decisions decisively. You don't shy away from a medical diagnosis, and you do what is necessary to provide your patients with the best treatment.

But somehow, when it comes to making financial decisions, you feel much less comfortable finalizing them and putting them into action. Why is that?

There are several potential reasons. Some of the ones reported by doctors include:

1. Not knowing where to start. Financial markets are confusing, chaotic, and inconsistent. It's like having to learn a different language, and regular intuition doesn't seem to apply

2. Not knowing whom to trust. The people offering you products and services all have their own agendas, and there's a lingering sense they may not have your best interests at heart

3. Feeling incompetent. Lack of knowledge makes us feel uncomfortable and vulnerable. Doctors are accustomed to having answers and being in control. Acknowledging financial incompetence feels like admitting to having a weakness

4. Discomfort with talking about money and financial decisions. In some cultures or families it's taboo to discuss money-related matters

Well, there's good news and bad news.

The bad news is that you *must* make financial decisions. Hopefully the earlier portions of this book covering the axioms and time value of money made it clear that procrastination is not an option. You must make some decisions early on, and you must make them competently—a lot is riding on it.

The good news is that you have the mental capacity to understand finance. The content may be annoying, it may be boring, and it may be voluminous (there's a lot of ground to cover), but it's not rocket science. It's nowhere as complex as pharmacological principles, reading an X-ray, or performing surgery.

Still on the good news: the *Pillars of Wealth* initiative (books, videos, face-to-face classes) is specifically designed to help you make better decisions. It provides you with basic knowledge on a wide range of financial topics, helping to build your confidence. Confidence makes it easier to make decisions and to deal with advisors, brokers, and agents.

Furthermore, discussing the material with your partner (assuming you have one) helps generate conversations that might otherwise be difficult to initiate. Once those conversations have taken place you can finally make decisions that have been put off—sometimes for far too long.

In this chapter I cover: two decision making paradigms, some psychological barriers that conspire to undermine our decision making, and first lines of defense (self-awareness and proactive preparation) against several well known dangers.

Decision Making Paradigms

For our purposes we'll consider two decision making paradigms: intuitive and rational.

Intuitive decisions are those we arrive at without conscious thought. Our brains assess circumstances and reflexively or impulsively 'recommend' courses of action. Such decisions are believed to be handled by the more ancient portions of our brains.

Rational decisions are the result of deliberate, conscious, thoughtful introspection. The poster child for rational decision making is Star Trek's Mr. Spock. Rational thought appears to take place in the newer portions of our brain: the frontal lobe, sometimes also referred to as the 'executive brain.'

According to the field of *evolutionary psychology*, we (humans) evolved simple intuitive decision making to help us react quickly to dangers and uncertainty. One example is the very basic instinctive choice we make between fleeing and fighting. But our surroundings in the last 5,000 years (and especially in the last 200 years) are very different from those we encountered over hundreds of thousands of years of evolution. This means our evolved intuition may not apply to current circumstances.

More than ever, we need our rational brain to override the impulsive inclinations triggered by intuition. Our failure to do so is manifested in our tendency to prefer overly simplistic explanations, blanket statements, and generalizations. Unfortunately, our fast paced lives and attention-deficit-disordered media reinforce "jumping to conclusions" and "keeping it simple stupid." Instead, we should recognize that the answers to most finance and economics questions should begin with a more thoughtful and nuanced, "It depends, ..."

The remaining portions of this chapter aim to help us elevate thoughts from the subconscious into the conscious, thereby allowing us to replace reflexive decisions with more thoughtful ones.

Psychological Barriers to Decision Making

Medical practitioners make important (sometimes life saving) decisions each day. Doctors are able to consistently make good decisions because they are (1) objective and (2) highly trained professionals.

Yet when it comes to financial decisions, doctors (and most other humans) make many mistakes, the majority of them avoidable. Why this susceptibility?

A big part of the answer is human psychology. Our psychological biases put us in danger, because:

1. They lead us to impulsively jump to incorrect conclusions, and
2. We're often unaware the biases are present—they operate in our subconscious

This combination often makes us our own worst enemy.

One psychological tendency I've already mentioned is procrastination, which often arises due to our psychological need to escape anxiety. When something that causes us anxiety comes up—

for example, the need to grapple with a financial decision—our minds find relief by ignoring the need to make the decision, i.e., by putting the decision off. Needless to say, procrastination doesn't solve the problem—it merely pushes it off to a later date. When the problem inevitably comes up again, it causes even greater anxiety because we have even less time left to make the decision.

Below are some psychological biases and factors that affect our decision making. Many of these may be linked to our evolved inclination toward intuitive decision making.

Overconfidence and the Illusion of Control

In his book, *Your Money & Your Brain*, Jason Zweig addresses *overconfidence* when he states that "One of the most fundamental characteristics of human nature is to think we're better than we really are." As an example, in a roomful of 100 people, he notes that 75 percent will raise their hands when asked if they believe they are better than the average person in the room, regardless of what they're supposed to be better at: telling jokes, driving cars or playing basketball. Needless to say, it's impossible for 75 percent of people to consistently be above average. (As a side note, men tend to exhibit greater overconfidence than women).

We also show tremendous overconfidence when it comes to love and relationships. Statistics tell us that 50% of marriages will fail, but when asked about the probability of our own marriage failing (close to our wedding date) we all swear that our risk is at most 10% and most likely 0%.

In the financial decision making context, overconfidence leads us to believe we can consistently pick winning stocks, correctly estimate probabilities of complex events, and see real patterns in markets where no one else can.

As documented by Malcolm Gladwell in a *New Yorker* article, the *illusion of control* occurs when one's "confidence spills over from areas where it may be warranted … to areas where it isn't warranted at all."

People who are reasonably successful in other arenas often assume they'll be successful as investors. They believe their position in society somehow gives them an edge, which will inevitably lead to investing success. They invariably realize (often painfully) just how little control they have in financial markets.

The illusion that success or competence in one area implies success elsewhere has been dispelled in numerous scientific articles. Among the earliest contributors in the field were psychologists William Chase and Herbert Simon, who studied chess players and established that expertise in chess did not necessarily translate into expertise elsewhere.

Despite overwhelming evidence we seem unable to recognize our own overconfidence and to identify and shake the illusion of control. Often we believe that our actions give us control over financial markets when such confidence isn't based on reality.

As investors we may resort to superstitions such as consulting our horoscope or invoking a prayer before launching stock market transactions. Neither of these acts affects the probability of our investing success, but they make us feel more confident, convinced that divine intervention is now working on our behalf.

There are many analogies to this in sport. For example, a baseball pitcher may touch his cap three times before each pitch, while a batter may tap his bat against his shoes in a set sequence before setting up in the batter's box.

In the investing realm, professionals often take advantage of our tendency to fall for the illusion of control. Consider firms touting their latest online trading platforms. Their advertisements flash colorful, three-dimensional graphs, tables and heat maps intended to look glamorous and sophisticated. Their pitch is designed to plant in our minds the idea that their product will give us greater control over financial markets and an edge over everyone else. In reality, of course, none of this glitz helps us to make better investments—it only makes us believe the illusion that we are getting an advantage.

The Endowment Effect

The *endowment effect* refers to the observation that most people appear to place a higher value on an object or investment *after* they've taken possession of it. One example of this phenomenon has been documented by Ziv Carmon and Dan Ariely, in the *Journal of Consumer Research*. The researchers interviewed two groups of students who had expressed an interest in a lottery allocating scarce tickets to a Duke University playoff basketball game. One group was composed of students who failed to receive tickets through the lottery. When contacted by researchers, members of this group expressed a willingness to pay an average price of $166 per ticket. The other group was composed of students who did receive ticket allocations through the lottery. Members of this group expressed a willingness to sell their tickets for an average price of $2,411 per ticket.

The study confirmed the hypothesis that people attribute higher value to an asset they own than the value attributed to the identical asset by those who don't own it.

In the investing context, this at least partly explains why we're reluctant to sell assets we already own. In our minds we associate a high (possibly sentimental) value with these holdings and we don't want to part with them.

Another emotional effect which often makes us reluctant to sell assets is loss aversion.

Loss Aversion

In financial markets, we inevitably struggle with situations involving the decline in value of an asset. Our reluctance to sell (sometimes despite mounting losses) is referred to as *loss aversion*. When an asset's price declines, we are still influenced by a belief that its 'fair' value is higher, and we often decide to wait for the price to appreciate to a more 'appropriate' value before we sell (*fair* and *appropriate* here are subjective values on which we've fixated). Deferring the sale allows us to avoid the anxiety of formally recognizing the loss, which becomes final when we sell out the position. So we convince ourselves that if we just give it a bit more time, the price will recover. But as we wait, the price declines further and further.

Lenders also suffer from loss aversion. Consider a bank that lends money to a business, and then the business takes a turn for the worse. Rather than writing off the loan and walking away, the bank feels an obligation to recoup the initial loan and agrees to lend more to the bad borrower. The borrower then promptly proceeds to mismanage the second loan. Now the bank has lost even more money. The bank's loss aversion decision is often referred to as "throwing good money after bad."

The rational approach is to ignore past losses (sometimes referred to as 'sunk costs') in making current decisions, but psychologically that doesn't come naturally to us.

Value Attribution

In their book, *Sway: The Irresistible Pull of Irrational Behavior*, authors Ori and Rom Brafman define *value attribution* as "Our inclination to imbue a person or thing with certain qualities based on initial perceived value." For example, we're likely to conclude that an impeccably dressed advisor with an impressive office is more capable than a shabbily dressed fellow with a small dusty office. Similarly, we may believe a company with a beautifully designed annual report is a superior investment to a firm with a more basic document.

In the medical setting, we are predisposed to assume that a person with a white coat and stethoscope is an authority (on *everything*). Value attribution predisposes us to assume the professor from the more prestigious university *must* be correct; that the advisor with the larger portfolio must be superior; or that a stock tip is more credible when overheard at a country club as opposed to the YMCA. Jumping to conclusions based on such attributes can set us down the wrong path.

Our intuition often leads us to reflexively assume that financial advisors have some ability to pick investments. But the scientific evidence says otherwise. Just because the person has a glitzy computer terminal on his desk doesn't mean he can consistently predict interest rates, market movements, winning stocks, etc.

Confusing Causation and Correlation

Confusing *causation* and *correlation* is a very common mistake. Often, an observed event or action may appear to cause another, when in reality the two events simply happen to coincide. In the more extreme cases, causation moves in the opposite direction.

Here's an example. Suppose your wise investments have led to a significant amount of wealth and you now wish to pursue your life's true passion: owning a race car team. You want to create the best team, one that will dominate the field for years to come. You decide that two necessary ingredients for success include a talented driver and a superior engine design. You begin a search and come across a very successful driver. A bit more investigation leads you to learn that he drives a vehicle with an innovative engine design.

Your budget allows you to do one of two things: hire the driver or license the engine design. You decide that the real key to the driver's success is the engine design. Based on this conclusion, you proceed to license the engine technology and seek to find a less expensive driver elsewhere. In making this decision, you've assumed causation: the engine *caused* the driver's racing success. But what if causation took a different path? What if the engine design looked flashy, but in reality did not provide any meaningful racing advantage? What if the flashy engine actually caused a slight disadvantage to a driver? What if the driver's unusual skill allowed him to win races *despite* the engine design? That is, the driver's skill *caused* racing success, not the engine. Needless to say, interpreting causation correctly is hugely important as it guides you to make the correct decision about whether to invest in the driver or engine.

Confusing the causation interpretation even further, it's conceivable that neither the engine nor the driver is the primary cause of the team's success. It's possible that the pit crew and team manager are the ones who consistently provide the team an advantage that leads to victory. Under this interpretation, there's no causal relationship at all between the engine and victory or the driver and victory; rather, the engine and driver merely *correlate* with victory.

Clearly, mistaking causation and correlation can be very damaging in the world of financial decision making, and in particular during investing decisions. We often buy stocks due to an (incorrect) assumption that we understand what drives their value. Subsequently, we're disappointed to find that the assumed relationship doesn't hold and our investments lose value. In our complex financial markets, it's possible to find many relationships between observed variables and stock price movements. The problem in most cases is that these relationships may be fleeting, or may reflect correlation but not causation. Nevertheless, our intuition leads us to assume causality, thereby putting our money at risk.

Selective Confirmation or Diagnosis Bias

When we selectively seek evidence to confirm our preconceived notions and beliefs, rather than accepting all evidence regardless of where it points us, we are guilty of *selective confirmation* (or *diagnosis bias*). As an example of selective confirmation bias, an investor who is committed to a particular strategy may point to historical observations that are consistent with her strategy and its prospects for success. Without consciously realizing it, the investor may have highlighted only those outcomes that matched her preconceived notions about market movements and investment value changes. By ignoring similar investments with *opposite* outcomes, she *selected* the evidence to match her beliefs. Since the evidence embraced is not objective, it's likely to lead to poor conclusions about investments.

Medical professionals are well aware of the dangers of these biases, because they are ever present dangers in medical research settings. Researchers tend to become attached to their hypotheses and subconsciously filter evidence to match their preconceived notions. But while medical professionals are well aware of diagnosis bias, they generally aren't on guard for psychological biases during financial planning. This undermines the quality of their financial decisions.

Inexperience

Inexperience is not a psychological bias, but it does affect the quality of decision making. By definition, beginner or amateur investors lack the experiences of professional investors. This deficiency makes it harder for them to make good decisions. For example, they may initiate a quick, impulsive investment without having a complete sense of what is going on.

We can link this discussion to the notion of intuition. Neuroscientists view intuition as a pattern-seeking process in which past experiences stored in the brain's 'database' are matched with current situations. Within this analogy, inexperience is the same as having a small database. The smaller the database, the fewer good matches can be found.

More than most professions, physicians understand the importance of building a large store of knowledge and developing intuition. Internships and residencies are geared to providing intense and complex exposure to medical ailments and treatments. Immediate feedback from senior colleagues increases the rate of learning, helping young doctors to create large brain databases.

But as part time investors, doctors don't get that intense learning with immediate feedback. This means their investing databases are sparse, making them more likely to make mistakes.

In some sense, the worst case situation arises when an inexperienced person has early success as an investor. This is because his small database then has very skewed experiences which further boost his overconfidence, making him more likely to believe he has an ability to see patterns in chaotic financial markets.

We see lack of experience all the time in the context of financial bubbles. Any person who began investing *after* the last bubble burst has no memory of the downturn, and therefore no memory of the anxiety and losses that take place during downturns. The longer it takes for a bubble to form, the larger the cohort of people whose databases lack sobering experiences.

The Dot com bubble which burst in 2000 and the home ownership bubble which slid off a cliff around 2008 both formed over the course of six or so years. In each case, this meant that tens of thousands of young investment bankers, traders, financial advisors, risk managers, brokers, loan officers, insurance agents and mid-level managers had never experienced a serious loss.

In their collective store of patterns, 'up' was the only possible outcome. Perhaps the appropriate cliché here is, "The bigger the cohort, the farther it falls." The larger the cohort of investors who feel invincible, the bigger the bubble, and the deeper the crash when their mortality is revealed.

Biological Factors

Decision making takes place within the brain, and therefore anything that affects the brain affects our decisions.

Our brain functions may be adversely affected by aging, disease or other physiological factors such as fatigue or chemical imbalance and depletion. Any of these may lead to sub-optimal decision making.

First Lines of Defense

Marketing experts at financial services firms know we're susceptible to psychological biases and inexperience, and they shamelessly take advantage in their advertising.

Our first lines of defense are *awareness* and *advance preparation*. Being aware of our psychological susceptibilities puts us on alert. This allows us to employ some healthy skepticism when approached by various salespeople.

Advance preparation reduces the decision making burden, because it forces us to think about major issues in advance and even to formulate some potential responses to shifting circumstances.

Medical professionals are acutely aware of the importance of being proactive. It's well known that preventative medicine is far more efficient and effective than reactive medicine. It's far better to fortify a patient in advance so that a disease or injury can be avoided than it is to pick up the pieces after the damage has occurred.

A solid first step is to anticipate and prepare for some of the predictable threats to your family's financial and emotional well being. These threats include:

1. Death (deprives family of breadwinner and a loved one)
2. Disability (deprives family of breadwinner)
3. Disaster (damages property and/or creates liability)
4. Disagreement with business partners (harms profitability)
5. Depression (reduces productivity)
6. Drug dependence (undermines trust and harms family unity)
7. Divorce (causes emotional and financial burdens)
8. Deception (embezzlement by partners or employees costs money and destroys trust)

You can buy insurance to mitigate the first three D's: death, disability, and disaster. Disagreement with business partners can be avoided or minimized through clear communication and drafting of a partnership or business agreement. Depression is a serious challenge for doctors, many of whom experience a lot of stress and often lack outlets for anxiety. Developing techniques for coping and communicating openly can help. These coping mechanisms can also help to avoid developing a dependence on prescription medications. Divorce can be mitigated proactively by knowing your prospective spouse and yourself well enough to make the right decision about who you marry, and then committing to nurture the relationship. Another proactive measure to insulate assets in the event of divorce is to insist on a prenuptial agreement. Deception in the workplace can be thwarted through business procedures that ensure oversight over sensitive business functions, including the handling of cash.

Final Thoughts on Decision Making

I'm going to indulge for a moment in the old fable of the race between the tortoise and hare.

The hare is fast, spontaneous and impulsive. But it ultimately loses the race to the slow, steady and committed tortoise. It may seem boring and unglamorous to act like the tortoise, but the evidence shows that a steady, unspectacular approach to financial planning tends to do better over the long-term. It also has the advantage of fewer emotional peaks and troughs.

A final thought: *a decision has not been made until you consciously take some action.* Thinking or dreaming about doing something doesn't count.

Once you've decided on a course of action—implement it!

Reviewing Your Employment Contract

A key theme in this book is that you should proactively anticipate and thwart risks. A lot of risk management takes place upfront in negotiating your employment contract or offer letter. Set yourself up for success by ensuring these are as favorable to you as possible.

Below is a list of common clauses you can expect to encounter in a typical employment agreement. Consult with a properly qualified and licensed attorney prior to signing any such documents.

Compensation

The contract should specify compensation, including base salary and any bonuses. It may also address annual increases to your base salary, which may or may not be automatic. It's reasonable to expect some cost of living adjustments to your base salary, to keep up with inflation.

Bonuses are often directly linked to productivity. For example, how many procedures you completed in a month or year.

Below are some compensation-related considerations.

Stark Law and Bonus Restrictions

According to the Stark Law, bonuses generally cannot be paid for Designated Health Services (DHS). Barry Rosen, a senior health care attorney at Baltimore's Gordon Feinblatt LLC, explains that the 'designated health services' covered by the Stark Law include:

1. Clinical laboratory services
2. Physical therapy, occupational therapy, and speech language pathology services
3. Radiology and certain other imaging services
4. Radiation therapy services and supplies
5. Durable medical equipment and supplies
6. Parenteral and enteral nutrients, equipment, and supplies
7. Prosthetics, orthotics, and prosthetic devices and supplies
8. Home health services
9. Outpatient prescription drugs
10. Inpatient and outpatient hospital services
11. Nuclear medicine

Your base salary can cover these activities, but you cannot receive a performance based bonus for them.

Employment Status

Your compensation (and benefits) may also depend on your employment status. As a private practice co-owner you may receive a salary, benefits, a bonus and a share in the profits of the practice. As an employee you can expect a salary, benefits, and perhaps a bonus. As an independent contractor you can expect a salary, and possibly a bonus. But benefits are unlikely to be included.

It's more favorable for a private practice to classify you as an independent contractor. Contractor status likely makes you ineligible for benefits, so the private practice's overhead costs are reduced. To some extent, contractor designation makes you a second class citizen compared to those with formal full time employment. Think carefully before accepting a contractor role.

Accounting Choices

Your employer will elect to keep its books using one of two accounting methods. These are known as *accrual* and *cash* accounting.

> *The cash method of accounting … records revenue when cash is received, and expenses when they are paid in cash, in contrast to the alternative accrual method which records income items when*

they are earned and records deductions when expenses are incurred regardless of the flow of cash. – Wikipedia

In plain English, the cash method records *actual* movements of cash, while the accrual method *assumes that money has moved* (into or out of the firm) when a contract for services has been signed or an invoice for payment has been received. The bottom line for you is that these two approaches can lead to different net income or profit results for your employer, which in turn may affect your bonus payout. Most likely you won't be able to force the employer to switch from one method to the other, but you should understand which one is being used and how it affects your annual compensation.

Relative Value Units

Many hospitals base at least some compensation on Relative Value Units (RVUs). This is a Medicare concept. It's used to determine a physician's reimbursement for each service and procedure listed in Medicare's fee schedule. In your workplace the system may be used to determine your productivity (how hard you're working). Private practices rarely use RVUs.

Every procedure has an RVU value associated with it (the RVU values are adjusted every two years by Medicare). In 2019 there are wholesale changes coming to the Medicare payment mechanism, representing a significant future source of uncertainty for physicians.

How do RVUs work? At the end of a given year, hospital administrators will multiply the frequency of each procedure you performed by its RVU; they will then sum those products up to yield a total RVU (for each physician) for the year. It's usually necessary to subtract from the total RVU some baseline amount to cover overhead expenses, then multiply that net RVU count by a net multiplier (a dollar rate per RVU) to yield the dollar bonus. The net multiplier is based on a Medicare compensation rate per RVU, net of overhead per RVU. So if the (gross) multiplier per RVU is $80, and the per RVU overhead is $30, the net multiplier is $50 dollars per RVU.

Let's say the total RVU count for the doctor in a given year is 30,000 Units, with a baseline of 25,000. In this case the productivity increase above the base is 5,000 RVU, and multiplying that by $50 yields a $250,000 bonus.

Independent of the RVU system, some people are paid on an 'eat what you kill' model where the physician receives some share of the revenue generated, net of overhead. According to Barry Rosen, there are different overhead formulas in use, some of which are more fair than others, and some of which create less constructive behavior. For example, there may be an incentive to get other departments to bear unfair amounts of the overhead. This can lead to conflict.

An efficient and fair system is one in which each specialist in a group performs the procedures she is good at. Done properly, this can lift the entire group's performance, resulting in higher net earnings for the group. But some incentives may lead physicians to compete internally over the provision of certain procedures, reducing efficiencies and overall earnings.

To determine whether your compensation offer is competitive, you can refer to compensation survey results. Medscape and the MGMA compile compensation data for physicians and private medical practices. The ADA compiles revenue, expense, and net income data for dental practices (see Resources list at the end of this book).

Benefits

Your employment contract should address all the usual benefits, including:

- Health insurance
- Disability and Life insurance
- Defined benefit or defined contribution pension plans
- Vacation allowance
- Legal insurance
- Coverage or on-call duties, and
- Children's college tuition benefits

Your human resources representative should be able to direct you to information on health insurance plan(s). Choose the plan and options that best meet your family's needs.

Disability and Life insurance policies offered through employers' group plans may offer limited benefits. Consider supplementing these group plans with your own private policies. These are discussed further in the Insurance chapter.

Make sure you understand whether you'll be participating in a *defined benefit* plan or a *defined contribution* plan. With defined benefit plans the employer guarantees you certain benefits in the future. With defined contribution plans, you shoulder the risk for the underlying investment performance. These are discussed in greater detail in the Pillars of Wealth chapter, under the heading 'Precarious Pillars.'

Make sure you're being offered a fair amount of vacation time. This is your opportunity to unwind from a stressful job and spend quality time with family and friends.

Your employer may also offer legal insurance. This could cover legal expenses for estate planning, debt collection, identity theft defense, tax audits, and the purchase, sale, and refinancing of a home.

The agreement should outline your coverage or on-call duties. While very senior doctors may be able to have these reduced or waived, more junior professionals are usually required to make themselves available for these additional duties. Having said that, you do have a right to ask that your required commitment be equitable. That is, you will not be required to take on a greater burden than others with similar seniority.

A benefit for doctors working in university hospitals is that their children may be eligible for significant reductions in college tuition. To be eligible, they must attend a school that is on an approved list.

Some (usually senior) employees may also be eligible for deferred compensation benefits. It's worthwhile to ask about these upfront to stake your claim in advance. These programs may involve the employer depositing some cash into a Trust and/or permanent insurance policy. The employee doesn't gain access to these plans for several years—usually at least five years. But the restriction also allows the contributed funds to benefit from tax advantages. Such arrangements are sometimes referred to as 'golden handcuffs,' and are used to secure long-term employment commitments from key employees.

Medical Malpractice Insurance

Patients or their survivors may initiate legal action against medical providers for bodily injury, mental anguish, medical expenses, and/or property damage.

Medical malpractice insurance (aka medical professional liability insurance or med-mal), is a type of insurance which protects medical professionals from liability associated with negligent or wrongful practices. The insurance may also cover the legal costs of defending against such claims.

Your employment contract should specify any medical malpractice insurance provided and the terms of that insurance. Since premiums for such insurance can be high, and claims can be overwhelming, this is one of the more important considerations in your contract.

A crucial consideration is whether the policy offered by the employer is based on *occurrence* or *claims-made*. According to the American College of Physicians (ACP),

> *"Claims-made" insurance protects you from malpractice claims only if the company that insured you at the time of the alleged "occurrence" is the same company at the time the claim is filed in court.*

If you had a claims-made policy and move to a different insurer (usually because you changed jobs), you need to purchase an insurance 'tail.' The tail (a onetime purchase) then provides protection for claims made on alleged incidents during which you used a different insurer. Buying the tail can be quite expensive when you leave an insurer. It can cost up to 2.5 times your previous annual premium. So if your annual malpractice insurance premium was $50,000, purchase of the tail could cost as much as $125,000.

Try to get your prospective (new) employer to agree to pay for the tail in the event you change jobs. Other arrangements may include having your current employer pay for the tail if your employment is terminated (you are fired), or you may have to pay if you decide to leave.

According to ACP, under an *occurrence* policy,

> *... any malpractice occurrence will be covered by the insurance carrier, provided it was the carrier at the time of the alleged event, regardless if it is the carrier at the time the claim is filed.*

With such a policy in place, you don't need the separate tail insurance.

In malpractice insurance policies, the insurer will usually pay for legal defense. Unlike most other insurance types, there may be no deductible requirement in such policies.

There are limits specified in medical malpractice policies. The insurer is only responsible for payments up to these limits. Any additional awards above and beyond must be made up from the assets of the practice or from the individual physicians' personal assets. This can be very damaging. Entire practices have been wiped out by liability awards in excess of insurance. It behooves you to know how much coverage your employer will provide to you, and you must gauge whether that is likely to protect you sufficiently.

One big consideration is whether the defense costs are included in the legal liability limit or are outside the limit. The latter is more favorable for you, as it leaves more funds available to cover a potential award.

Statutes of limitations on actions taken on medical malpractice grounds can vary widely. On the high end they can be up to 21 years for pediatricians (limitation for them is 3 years after the minor becomes an adult). With such a long span of time over which liability persists, it's necessary to ensure you have appropriate protection in place. Make sure the conditions in your contract are explained to you by a qualified attorney!

Ignoring these issues can mean putting some of your pillars of wealth in danger.

There are numerous resources on the topic of professional liability. The *New England Journal of Medicine* provides the article: "Malpractice Risk According to Physician Specialty." There's information available on the Practice Management section of the American College of Physicians website. The American Medical Association publishes the book: *The Physician Professional Liability Market and Regulatory Environment*.

Termination Circumstances

You may want to ensure that termination circumstances are clearly spelled out in your employment contract. This can provide you with protection against being fired unfairly. Of course, with specific circumstances detailed in your contract, there's a good chance you'll lose your job without any recourse if you fail to live up to your responsibilities.

Be on the lookout for overly onerous termination clauses. For example, suppose you're being told your contract is for two years, but there's a clause stating you can be terminated with 60 days notice. In reality, you don't have a two year contract—you have a 60 day contract! You could conceivably move your entire household to some remote region, only to be given notice that in 60 days your employment will terminate. To protect against this, you could request that the 60 day notice clause can only be triggered after one or two full years of service.

Non-Compete & Non-Solicitation

One of the major dangers to a medical practice is that key employees will defect to nearby competitors or set up their own competing entity in the same neighborhood. A popular physician or dentist can poach a large number of clients, severely harming the original practice.

To address these risks, employers will usually include non-compete and non-solicitation clauses. A non-compete clause typically forbids you from setting up shop within a certain radius of the existing practice over some period of time. A non-solicitation clause aims to stop you from taking the original practice's clients.

These clauses cannot be overly restrictive as this is deemed to unfairly harm employees' ability to make a living.

If you do leave and your former employer is concerned that you have breached these clauses, the former employer may seek *injunctive relief* through the court system—seeking to force you to stop or restrict your new activities.

You need a competent attorney who can provide guidance on which non-compete/non-solicitation conditions are likely to be accepted by the courts and which may be thrown out or amended.

As an employer, the last thing you want is for a judge to throw out all your non-compete and non-solicitation conditions on the grounds that they are unfair, as this could mean that your former employees may then be free to open up shop across the hall from you and take all your clients!

Integration & Fraud

Integration refers to the concept that the agreement you sign represents the entire agreement, and verbal promises made prior to that are not part of the agreement (for example, separate promises about signing bonus, moving allowance, etc.).

There are often clauses that specify that "this is the entire agreement..." but even without such language the integration concept applies.

There is an exception to the integration concept if the original promises made to the employee (prior to provision of the contract) were made with the explicit intention of *not* honoring them. In such cases the other party (employer) has acted fraudulently. But it's very difficult to prove such 'intent'.

In some states, if the employer fails to reveal material information when it offers you a contract, for example, that the practice is currently under investigation, you may have grounds for legal action. This may be the case even in the absence of a (misleading) clause in the agreement explicitly stating "we are not under investigation."

Indemnification

Indemnification is an agreement to protect another party from injury or loss. In practical terms, indemnification clauses in employment agreements usually state that the offending party must cover the injured party's losses, which may include attorney fees.

Business Ownership

Some employment agreements allow for the possibility of acquiring an ownership stake in the practice. You should think carefully about whether you really want to be an owner. Does being an owner provide a meaningful difference in compensation, including prospects for *dividends* (sharing in the profits of the business)? How much say will you have in running the practice? Do you want to have a say? How much will it cost you to buy into the practice? Is it worth it to pay that much to buy in given what you believe are the compensation prospects down the road as an owner? Do you have to take on some liabilities or obligations as a partner or owner and do you want those liabilities? What exactly will your role be as co-owner? Is there a small clique in place with ultimate control? Will you be able to influence decisions? How important is that to you?

The practice likely won't *guarantee* you an ownership path. Instead, it will allow you to be *considered* for ownership if you meet certain requirements and triggers. The contractual trigger to ownership may be based on time (seniority) and/or revenue raised (for example, you may have to prove you can bring in a million dollars of revenue a year). Another trigger may be a specified increase in the entire practice's revenues.

If you do become an owner is there an exit mechanism? Is there a process in place dictating how your equity stake is to be returned to the remaining owners? How much do you get for your share? Will you still be responsible for certain liabilities or obligations? Will you have to agree to a non-compete in the event you leave and how onerous will that be? Can you be ousted and forced to leave, and if so, what severance would you be entitled to?

Final Thoughts on Employment Contracts

Invariably, physicians are told that hiring an attorney to examine employment contracts is a good idea. Inevitably, some elect not to take that advice. Yes, it can seem difficult to justify a $1,500 expense for a contract lawyer when you're earning a resident's salary, carrying a heavy debt load and trying to figure out how to cover your family's moving expenses to a new location. But there is a compelling reason to spend the money.

Your first contract often sets the bar and determines your subsequent contract terms. Accepting an unfavorable contract early on can mean years spent trying to catch up. It's usually much cheaper in the long run to secure the services of an attorney and get a more favorable contract, rather than having to play catch-up for several years in an effort to make up lost ground.

In hindsight, many physicians wish they'd spent the money to strike a much better deal.

Furthermore, the attorney can be deputized as your negotiator, allowing her to take a harder stance, while you can separately maintain a collegial tone with your future colleagues.

You may not get all the changes you request during contract negotiations, but you can and should always ask—politely.

An administrator is likely to hand you a contract and state upfront that it's the "standard contract offered to all prospective employees." Many young doctors interpret this (as intended) to mean that it's non-negotiable. In some cases it's true that the entry level contract is non-negotiable. But in other cases there may be room for negotiation—the administrator is simply hoping that you'll jump to the aforementioned conclusion.

It costs you nothing to respond politely with a request for changes or additions to the contract. The worst thing that can happen is that the employer will say 'no.' But if you don't try, you may be leaving a lot of value on the table.

Estate Planning – Transferring Pillars to Others

Estate planning is the process of accumulating, managing, conserving and transferring wealth, taking into account tax and legal considerations. In this chapter we cover basic estate planning documents including Wills, Trusts, and Advance Health Care Directives. We also discuss tax and asset protection planning.

In the context of our pillars of wealth discussion, estate planning helps us to protect and grow our pillars and to make plans for transferring them to heirs, charitable organizations, etc.

You work hard to build a family and support it with pillars of wealth. You don't want to see those pillars damaged and reduced in value. Reductions may come about due to: avoidable taxation, litigation due to malpractice or internal family feuds, theft, poor investment performance, poor private practice results, … it's a long list.

Regardless of the cause, you owe it to yourself and your family to make good estate planning choices. Attorney Thomas Sessa points out that under some circumstances, drafting a Will that leaves everything to a spouse may not be the best choice. This is a reminder that what we think is the obvious estate planning move may in some cases be less than ideal.

Estate planning can be very complex. Consult a qualified and properly licensed attorney to ensure your estate planning documents are appropriate to your needs and circumstances, and consistent with the laws of your home state.

Basic Estate Planning Documents

When a person passes away, the default process for disposition of assets is known as *probate*. More specifically, probate is the process of gathering the assets owned by the deceased, paying creditors, distributing the net assets to beneficiaries and reporting all those transactions to a court of law. Put another way, probate is the legal process of changing and recording transfer of ownership for assets that have no other mechanism for such title changes.

The probate process helps heirs to cleanly secure ownership of inherited assets. It also protects creditors. But the process can be expensive and complex. There's also a loss of privacy as assets disposed of through the probate process are recorded and the records are made available to the public.

Intestacy is another term that's useful to keep in mind. It refers to the state of affairs that prevails when a person dies without a Will, i.e., without the instructions for disposition of assets. As already noted, when this happens, state probate laws govern how assets are distributed.

As estate related laws continuously change and evolve over time, attorney Michaela Muffoletto recommends completely rewriting estate planning documents at least once every ten years. It's important to redraft estate planning documents after major life events such as birth of a child, marriage, divorce, etc. Since estate related laws are state-specific, it's also necessary to revisit such documents after a move to a different state.

A Will

According to Thomas Sessa, a Will takes effect upon a person's death, and serves as an instruction guide for the probate process. The existence of a properly executed Will means that instead of the default court-governed process, a person's specific wishes will be followed for disposition of any assets that are in that person's own/sole name. This applies only to those assets that don't already have a designated beneficiary.

Assets that already have a beneficiary designated—for example, life insurance and retirement plans such as 401(k), 403(b), and IRA— don't need to be specified in the Will to determine their ownership when a person dies. That is, these assets don't need to go through probate.

Trusts

A Trust is a legal arrangement in which property is transferred by a *grantor* to a *trustee*. The trustee conserves and manages the transferred property for the benefit of any named beneficiaries. Typically, the grantor is a parent and the beneficiaries are that parent's spouse and/or children. The trustee may be a family member or a professional. Professional trustees must be paid.

Trust-related laws are state-specific and can be quite complex. If constructed improperly, some or all of their intended benefits may not hold up legally. You should seek competent legal advice in drafting any Trust documents.

While prices differ across states and depend on the complexity of each Trust, a ballpark figure is that a basic Trust is likely to cost somewhere between $3,000 to $5,000 to set up. Thereafter, ongoing annual costs may apply, including annual payments to the trustees who oversee the operation of the Trust and accountants who file annual tax returns on behalf of the Trust. In most states, it's typical to appoint a family member as trustee, often without any payment. Annual tax filing for basic Trusts usually costs less than $1,000.

Revocable Trust

A *Revocable Trust* is one which the grantor may access and change over time. That is, the grantor can revoke earlier instructions and replace them with new ones. A Revocable Trust (or Living Trust) avoids the probate process and its related costs but the assets in the Trust are included in the grantor's estate and will be subject to federal tax. In some ways a Revocable Trust is effectively a Will substitute: a private instruction book for disposition of assets. The Trust holds all properly titled assets and provides instructions for their disposition. These details are *not* made public.

Irrevocable Trust

The assets transferred into an *Irrevocable Trust*, as the name implies, cannot be withdrawn by the grantor. Once the grantor transfers assets into this type of Trust, she generally loses control of those assets. The loss of control has an upside, in more favorable tax treatment. Since the assets are no longer under the grantor's control, they're not included in the grantor's estate upon death. This can be used to reduce income and estate taxes and to protect assets from creditors.

Pour-Over Will

A *Pour-over Will*, in conjunction with a previously prepared Revocable Trust, puts all relevant assets into the Trust upon death. To avoid probate on any of these assets, however, it's necessary (in advance of death) to *re-title* them (assign the title or ownership of those assets to the Trust). The Revocable Trust ends up holding all properly titled assets. Any assets that were not properly re-titled to the Trust in advance are still passed on to the Trust as stated in the Will, but they don't avoid probate, which means they are publicly recorded.

Testamentary Trust

A *Testamentary Trust* is usually made within a Will (note the connection to the full expression: *Last Will and Testament*). The Trust is typically created to hold assets for minors, and specifies when and how much of the underlying assets may be distributed. Those triggers are often age based.

The Trust comes into being upon the death of the grantor. The grantor is the person whose assets are being disposed of in the Will.

Advance Health Care Directive

Living Will and Health Care Agent Designation are separate legal documents. They are sometimes combined into an Advance Health Care Directive.

The *Living Will* contains instructions for end of life decisions (all of which apply *prior* to death). For example, what type of care should be provided to you, and under what circumstances should certain medical procedures be attempted or not attempted. The Living Will should not be confused with a Will, which governs what will happen to assets *after* death.

The *Health Care Agent Designation* (HCAD) designates a person who is authorized to make decisions on your behalf. This agent is usually a spouse or adult child.

The designated Agent is expected to follow any instructions you provided, but may also be granted the authority to change your choices. The point for this power is that circumstances may change and it can be important for the agent to have the flexibility to make decisions you could not have anticipated in your original instructions.

As noted above, in some states the Living Will and Health Care Agent Designation may be combined into a single document, referred to as an *Advance Health Care Directive* (AHCD).

The AHCD avoids a situation of guardianship by the public legal system over a *person* (we're assuming that person is you). It's much better to have these important decisions made by a trusted and loving relative or friend rather than the rigid, public and expensive court system.

Financial Power of Attorney

Even if you're no longer competent to make financial decisions, there are still bills to be paid and investment decisions to be made. The Financial Power of Attorney (FPOA) allows a designated person (agent) to initiate banking and other financial transactions on behalf of the incompetent person (assumed to be you).

The FPOA is typically made effective even while you are not incompetent! Obviously this creates the risk that a person may abuse that power, so why are these typically made effective while you are competent? The answer has to do with convenience. If the power only takes effect when you are deemed incompetent, a financial institution could challenge the designated power holder's authority by arguing that you are, in fact, still competent. This could tie up any decisions in legal wrangling, stopping the designated agent from making important decisions for you. To avoid the debate and related delays, it's easier (not necessarily better) to have the FPOA in effect in advance.

The FPOA avoids a situation of guardianship by the public legal system over *property* (we're assuming that property is yours). It's generally better to have family or a trusted friend making financial decisions rather than these being controlled through public and costly court proceedings.

Tax Planning

In this section we highlight a few tax planning considerations which tend to apply to medical professionals. Given space constraints we cannot address tax issues comprehensively. Tax-related decisions should be undertaken with the advice of a competent CPA or tax attorney. Note that minimizing one's tax bill should be pursued legally. *Avoiding* taxes through legal means is perfectly legitimate. *Evading* taxes that should be paid is illegal.

As a general statement, the goal of tax planning is to minimize one's tax bill, and this can often be achieved by deferring taxes as far into the future as possible.

The typical doctor's primary asset is a large retirement plan, often in the form of a 401(k), 403(b), or IRA account. After 30 or more years of employment, such accounts can easily contain several million dollars. Given the amounts of money at stake it's important to set up retirement accounts in a way that ensures tax advantages to your spouse and next generations are maximized. Improper setup can limit the long-term benefit of these accounts.

Let's use an example in which a male doctor with an IRA account containing $1 million has named his wife as beneficiary. Upon his death, the spouse can roll over ownership of that IRA into her own name. Subsequently, it's as though she was the owner of the account all along, and she can elect how she would like to receive the proceeds (subject to some rules specifying required minimum distributions from retirement accounts).

The spouse can then elect to use a Stretch IRA to pass the proceeds of the account to her children over *their* expected lifetimes. The expected lifetime calculations depend on the recipients' current ages and their demographically-determined life expectancies. So a fifty-five year old child who is determined (using the government's formulas) to have a life expectancy of 25 years may be able to 'stretch' receipt of the IRA assets over 25 years. In this simplified example those amounts would be on the order of $1 million divided by 25 = $40,000 annually. Under this mechanism the doctor's children get to reset the account distributions to their remaining life expectancies. But this option is only available for one generation. In the event the aforementioned child passes away after ten years, his children (the doctor's grandchildren) don't get a reset. Instead, they would likely only be allowed to stretch receipt of the IRA proceeds over the remaining 15 years.

If an IRA does not specify any surviving beneficiaries, the funds end up in the doctor's estate, and must be withdrawn within 5 years. One million dollars received over 5 years means withdrawals of approximately $200,000 annually. Such amounts would likely increase the recipient's marginal tax rate—a tax planning failure.

In the most extreme case, the beneficiary may have an urgent need for funds. Withdrawing a million dollars at once (all of which is added to the recipient's taxable earnings) would trigger taxes at the highest marginal tax rates—arguably the worst-case scenario from a tax planning perspective.

There are other ways to approach the tax planning challenge by naming a Trust as the beneficiary of a qualified account. Upon death the account becomes re-titled to the Trust. Under the correct arrangements, your human beneficiaries can still get the stretch benefits while simultaneously enjoying traditional Trust protections and control over disbursements. Various formalities must be observed for such arrangements to be legally acceptable. Therefore, it's highly advisable to review all these decisions and structures with a competent and specialized attorney and tax accountant.

According to attorney Sessa, the big joke during his law school years was that nearly all of ERISA (the legal act which applies to retirement accounts) was in response to 'creative' ways in which physicians saved for retirement. The relevant observation for us is that 'creative' plans are likely to run afoul of the law, leading to significant legal and financial liability.

Another way to avoid taxes is to give assets to charity. Suppose you own stocks that have appreciated significantly over the years. If you sell them you will likely trigger significant capital gains taxes. These can be avoided by gifting those appreciated assets to a charity.

Other tax-favored financial choices may include investments in *municipal bonds* (bonds issued by state, city or county governments). Due to the legal separation between state and federal powers, the federal government can't impose taxes on interest paid by municipalities. In some cases residents of a state are also exempt from paying state taxes on local state bonds. The higher a person's marginal tax rate, the higher the benefit from receiving federal- or state-tax exempt interest payments. Of course, the decision to invest in municipal bonds must also take into consideration the risks and returns one can expect, as well as any diversification potential across all other invested assets.

Another financial tool that has the potential for avoiding some taxation is life insurance. Death benefit proceeds are generally income-tax free to named beneficiaries (but not necessarily estate-tax free). Life insurance is discussed in greater detail in a subsequent chapter.

There can also be significant tax implications associated with real estate. Some tax benefits are related to how long a person has owned property and whether it's a primary residence.

Finally, there are tax implications when receiving interest and dividends and selling financial securities for a capital gain or loss. Since taxes on short-term capital gains (assets held less than a year) are higher than on long-term capital gains (assets held more than a year), the timing of asset sales can be very important.

Asset Protection Planning

Asset protection refers to keeping one's assets safe from being claimed by creditors. Creditors are people or entities who are owed money, including those who have been awarded malpractice or other legal awards.

According to attorney Wayne Zell, asset protection planning is extremely important for medical practitioners and in particular for those practicing in fields that are susceptible to malpractice suits.

There are a number of tools that can be used to protect assets. Here we briefly discuss: pension and retirement investment accounts, malpractice insurance, irrevocable trusts, titling assets as tenants by the entirety, homesteads, asset protection and offshore trusts, prenuptial agreements, and life insurance and annuity contracts. A given tool may be effective against specific creditor categories but not others, and protections may not be absolute.

Pension and Retirement Investment Accounts

Generally, pension assets and qualified investment accounts such as 401(k) plans are protected from bankruptcy creditors. Roth and Traditional IRAs also have some protection, as do 403(b) accounts.

There are some exceptions and limits to these protections so make sure you're obtaining advice from an expert.

Malpractice Insurance

According to Anupam B. Jena, et al., in a *New England Journal of Medicine* (2011) article spanning 1991-2005 malpractice claim data:

> *Across specialties, 7.4% of physicians annually had a claim ... There was significant variation across specialties in the probability of facing a claim, ranging annually from 19.1% in neurosurgery, 18.9% in thoracic–cardiovascular surgery, and 15.3% in general surgery to 5.2% in family medicine, 3.1% in pediatrics, and 2.6% in psychiatry.*

The article proceeds to quantify the average award paid to claimants: "Across specialties, the mean indemnity payment was $274,887, and the median was $111,749."

Clearly, malpractice is a serious risk, and insurance against malpractice exposure is a necessary part of any doctor's risk management toolkit. With proper protection, the insurance company will pay your attorney fees and any judgments against you, instead of the funds coming from your personal assets (your pillars). Malpractice insurance is discussed in the Employment Contract and Insurance chapters of this book.

Irrevocable Trusts

Irrevocable Trusts are discussed earlier in this chapter. The key with such Trusts is that the grantor is required to give up control of any assets placed in the Trust. Since the grantor has effectively given these assets away, they now irrevocably belong to the Trust. While a doctor may be found liable professionally or personally, a Trust (a distinct legal entity) that's outside the doctor's control is not automatically guilty of any wrongdoing or malpractice. Therefore, as the logic goes, the Trust's assets should not be available to creditors.

Tenancy by the Entirety

This is a form of joint ownership of an asset which only applies to married couples. *Tenancy by the Entirety* has a crucial condition—that neither owner alone can 'sever' the joint tenancy. Let's assume the jointly owned asset in question is a real estate property. In plain English this means that neither spouse can make a unilateral decision to sell, donate, give as a gift or otherwise convey their share of the property to another person. Property held in this way may be protected from creditors of one spouse on the grounds that it's unfair to financially damage the other (presumed innocent or non-liable) spouse.

Tenancy by the Entirety may not be recognized in all states.

Homesteads

Legally, a *homestead* is a house (and land) in which a family resides. The family home may have some protection from creditors. These rules vary significantly from state to state, ranging from very significant protections, to no protections at all.

Asset Protection Trusts & Offshore Trusts

Some states, such as Delaware and Alaska, offer *Asset Protection Trusts*, which may be available for non-residents. Under some conditions, asset protection Trusts may provide a higher level of protection than traditional in-state Trusts, but they are also more expensive.

One may pursue even greater asset protection by arranging for an *Offshore Trust*, i.e., a Trust set up under the laws of another country. Offshore Trusts can be extremely expensive to set up and therefore only likely to be relevant for wealthier households.

In this discussion we're focusing on asset protection. Offshore trusts are often viewed suspiciously as efforts to evade taxes and therefore come under greater scrutiny by US officials. Accordingly, attorney Thomas Sessa urges that you have a "highly, highly, highly, competent attorney and accountant in handling offshore assets."

Prenuptial Agreements

Prenuptial or premarital agreements (often referred to as *prenups*) are contracts entered into prior to marriage or civil union which outline the disposition of assets, spousal support and guardianship over children.

Prenups are not enforceable in all 50 states.

An obvious challenge when it comes to such agreements is that the mere suggestion is often viewed as a lack of commitment to the relationship.

The romantic vision of marriage is one of equality. Prenups tend to favor the partner who has more assets and create an uncomfortable situation in which one spouse is "more equal than the other."

Wayne Zell adds that another challenge is that after signing well-drafted agreements, couples often inadvertently commingle assets (for example, buy property or open a bank account jointly)—actions which typically defeat the purpose of separation of ownership dictated by the agreement in the first place.

Life Insurance & Annuities

In some states (but not all), life insurance policies and/or annuity contracts have some asset protection features. For example, the cash value of permanent life insurance policies or the proceeds of annuities may be protected from creditors. Make sure you fully understand the protections available to you in your state.

According to Wayne Zell, placing a life insurance policy in an Irrevocable Trust (Irrevocable Life Insurance Trust or ILIT) can provide two layers of protection, as long as the Trust is properly drafted and administered. Such arrangements can also help to achieve income tax and estate planning objectives, making them potentially useful estate planning tools.

Final Thoughts on Asset Protection

Asset protection vehicles such as Trusts cannot be created, and assets cannot be transferred into them, *after* a legal claim such as a malpractice suit has been launched.

Moving assets into a Trust after a claim arises can be viewed as a fraudulent act (known as a *Fraudulent Conveyance*). The upshot is that once a claim has been filed, it's too late to create a Trust or move assets around. As in all proper risk management processes, the key is to be proactive and set up the asset protection Trust or other tools *in advance*.

If you set up an asset protection entity and there's a legal judgment against you, the assets inside the entity (for example, a Trust) may be out of reach of creditors. But if there are flows out of the protected vehicle (for example payments made out of the Trust), those flows may be subject to seizure.

According to attorney Barry Rosen, people sometimes spend so much time and effort on insulating assets from creditors that they hurt their spouse and heirs by constraining the mobility of assets and miss out on tax or other estate planning benefits they could have realized. While devastatingly large creditor claims do occur, they tend to be rare. It's important therefore to keep one's asset protection plans in proportion to the anticipated risks.

Final caution: Wayne Zell points out that personal assets may be placed in danger whenever a doctor enters into a contract that contains harsh language potentially imposing *personal* liability. Be on the lookout for these!

The American Health Care Industry

The American health care industry is complex. That may be the understatement of the century. A full treatment of the American health care system is well beyond the scope of this book. With this in mind we'll focus on a small number of high level concepts including the history and structure of health care in the United States, the roles of Medicare and Medicaid, the compensation mechanisms available to doctors, and recent information on the Patient Protection and Affordable Care Act (known as 'Obamacare'). The Republican administration set to take office in January, 2017 has vowed to repeal or drastically change this Act.

History of Health Insurance in the U.S.

In 1929, despite opposition from the American Medical Association (AMA), Baylor teachers in Dallas, Texas, formed Blue Cross to provide hospital care for their constituents (at a cost of 3 cents per day). This was the first prominent voluntary health insurance program and it spread throughout Texas and ultimately nationally. In 1939 the California Medical Society sponsored a plan (Blue Shield) to cover services offered by physicians in medical groups.

The concept of a national health insurance program gained importance in the 1930s. However, under pressure from the AMA and conservative congressmen, national health insurance provisions were stripped out of the Social Security Act by President Franklin D. Roosevelt in 1935.

After World War II fringe benefits such as health insurance were used by employers to attract employees. Private health insurance plans grew and began to compete with Blue Cross and Blue Shield.

In 1960, the Kerr-Mills Act created the Medical Assistance for the Aged (MAA) program which gave states the power to decide which patients needed financial (welfare) assistance. The federal government provided matching funds to the states for the program. Some states chose not to participate.

In 1965, two amendments were made to the Social Security Act of 1935: Medicare and Medicaid. Medicare had two parts: Part A, providing hospital insurance for the aged, and Part B, providing supplementary medical insurance. Medicaid was created as an entitlement program to help states provide medical coverage for low-income families and other individuals who met eligibility requirements. Currently, the federal Centers for Medicare and Medicaid Services (CMS) monitors and runs Medicare and Medicaid.

Structure of the American Health Care Industry

There are three main types of health insurance in the United States: (1) voluntary or private health insurance, (2) social health insurance, and (3) welfare insurance.

Voluntary Health Insurance

Voluntary health insurance consists of Blue Cross and Blue Shield, commercial health insurance companies and health maintenance organizations (HMOs).

Social Health Insurance

The two prominent social health insurance programs in the United States are Workers' Compensation and Medicare Part A. *Workers' Compensation* covers on-the-job injury or illness. Employers are generally required to provide Workers' Compensation coverage to employees. Coverage doesn't apply to non-work related ailments. Medicare is described further, below.

Welfare Insurance

Welfare medical services are provided by a web of providers at the local, state and federal levels. The most prominent is the federal government's Medicaid program, which is described further, below.

Medicare

Medicare is the main federal government entitlement program for health services in the United States. Medicare funds various medical services for those who are: 65 and over, disabled and eligible for Social Security benefits, or suffer from end-stage renal disease.

There are many common misunderstandings when it comes to Medicare coverage. One of these is the assumption that Medicare covers 'everything.' In fact, the most prevalent Medicare offering (known as Medicare Part A) only provides hospital insurance. Medicare Part B—supplementary medical insurance—is designed to complement Part A by covering various outpatient services and physician fees including many preventive services.

Notably, routine hearing and eye examinations as well as basic dental care are *not* covered by Part B.

Part C, known as Medicare Advantage, allows patients to receive medical services from Home Maintenance Organizations (HMOs).

Medicare Part D, prescription drug coverage, provides prescription drug plans designed to keep costs low.

Participation in Medicare Parts B, C, and D is voluntary and requires additional payments by patients.

Doctors generally enroll with Medicare as *participating physicians*, and must accept Medicare's terms. They can receive reimbursements from Medicare (under certain conditions) even if they're not formally enrolled as participating physicians. There are a variety of reimbursement mechanisms available across the range of Medicare services.

Hospital Reimbursement under Medicare

Prior to 1983, Medicare reimbursed hospitals on a fee-for-service basis for physician and related hospital services. Hospitals were reimbursed for any reasonable costs incurred, where *reasonable* was broadly defined. Since 1983, payment rates have been determined on a per case basis, in a system known as the Prospective Payment System (PPS) using Diagnosis Related Groups (DRGs) to classify cases for payment. That payment is based strictly on the DRG diagnosis.

Under PPS, payment to hospitals bears no direct relationship to the length of stay, services rendered or costs of care. When the designated PPS rate for a specific diagnosis is higher than actual costs, the hospital can keep the difference. If the hospital's actual costs exceed the PPS payment, the hospital absorbs the loss.

Medicaid

Medicaid provides a welfare structure for poor individuals and families. The funds are provided by the federal government, and the system itself is administered by individual states. The key for participating providers catering to the Medicaid population is that they must accept the fixed fee schedule for services imposed by Medicaid. Providers cannot charge more than Medicaid's fixed fees for a given procedure. Medicaid reimbursement rates are low compared to other insurance systems. Medical practices catering to Medicaid patients must therefore be highly efficient in order to achieve breakeven (and profitability).

Under Medicaid, individual states determine the scope of services offered, but they must provide at least: family planning, home health, physician, hospital outpatient, lab and X-ray, certified nurse practitioner, and nurse midwife services. They must also provide hospital inpatient care, nursing facilities, rural health clinics, early and periodic screening for children under 21, and medical and surgical services provided by a dentist.

Physician Compensation

The main compensation mechanisms available to doctors in the United States are salary, capitation and fee-for-service. These are described below.

Salary

Under the *salary* model, the provider is compensated for her time—not for productivity. That is, it doesn't matter how many patients are seen by a salaried physician or how many procedures that physician performs. Under this compensation model, the income level is set and physicians know in advance how much they'll earn per month or year.

There may be a separate bonus structure added to salary, which is tied to patient volumes or quality of care.

Salary or *salary plus bonus* (salary plus incentive) models are most often seen in large HMOs, academic settings, and large corporate- or physician-owned practices. A guaranteed salary, with or without bonus, is the most prevalent model today for new physicians. These salary models are designed to offer a sense of security for young physicians, by guaranteeing a minimum level of income.

Capitation

Under *capitation* (or prepayment) systems, doctors are paid based on the number of patients serviced over a specified period of time. For example, an insurer may provide to a medical practice the sum of $2,000 per patient over the course of a year to cover all office visits. Thus, a practice with 500 patients would have a budget of $1 million for that year. The doctors within that practice would have to control costs under this total revenue cap to ensure the practice's profitability and their own income.

The concept of capitation—prepaid health care premiums allocated to provider groups for all coverage or specialty-services coverage of a defined enrollee population—became more prevalent in the late 1980s and early 1990s. Capitation is intended to reward groups, and in turn those groups' individual physicians, who deliver cost-efficient, effective care.

The recently introduced *concierge model* of care falls under the capitation category.

Fee-for-Service

Under *fee-for-service* (FFS), the doctor is paid per service or procedure. The more procedures, the higher the revenue generated, and the higher the doctor's income.

Insurers may reimburse through: (1) a *fixed fee* schedule in which an insurer such as Medicaid pays the physician a non-negotiable fixed amount and the patient is not required to pay anything; (2) *indemnity*, in which a compensation amount is specified per procedure (and may vary across insurers), but the doctor can charge the patient more than the specified amount and keep the excess (the Relative Value Unit mechanism, discussed in the Employment Contract section of this book, is an example of indemnity and is common in hospitals); and (3) *service benefits*, which pay (per service or procedure) a percentage of "usual, customary and reasonable" (UCR) fees. For example, the provider may be reimbursed at 80% of the prevailing UCR fees. A co-pay may apply for the patient.

Many health policy experts believe that the FFS system must be adjusted because it currently rewards patient volume rather than care quality.

The Patient Protection and Affordable Care Act

In March 2010, President Obama signed a comprehensive health reform bill, the Patient Protection and Affordable Care Act (PPACA). The bill attempts to expand medical coverage, control health care costs and improve health care delivery. Below is a brief summary of the legislation as it stands currently. The incoming Republican administration which begins its term in 2017 has vowed to repeal or drastically change PPACA.

Expand Medical Coverage

One of the key components to the bill is the individual mandate which requires all US citizens and legal residents to have health care. To facilitate the purchase of health insurance, state-based health exchanges have been created through which individuals may purchase coverage. There are cost sharing credits available to individuals/families with income between 133-400% of the federal poverty level (FPL). To encourage participation, those without coverage pay a tax penalty.

Employers with 50 or more full-time employees must provide health insurance to their employees or tax credits enabling employees to buy insurance through a health exchange. Employers with more than 200 employees must offer health insurance plans and automatically enroll employees into those plans. An employer who fails to do this faces a fine per employee. Employers with fewer than 50 full-time employees are exempt from these penalties.

There is an overall expansion of the Medicaid program. Medicaid will cover all non-Medicare eligible individuals under age 65 (children, pregnant women, parents, and adults without dependent children) with incomes up to 133% of the FPL based on modified adjusted gross income. All newly eligible adults will be guaranteed a benchmark benefit package that meets the essential health benefits available through the exchanges.

PPACA mandates that states retain current income eligibility levels for parents of children covered under Medicaid and the Children's Health Insurance Program (CHIP) until 2019.

To further expand health care coverage, the bill states that insurance companies must provide dependent coverage for children up to age 26 in all individual and group policies. Private insurance companies can no longer rescind coverage or use pre-existing conditions as exclusions for children, except in cases of fraud. Furthermore, private insurers cannot place lifetime limits on the dollar value of coverage.

Control Health Care Costs

As a cost containment strategy, PPACA allows providers to organize as *Accountable Care Organizations* (ACOs) that can share in cost savings they achieve for the Medicare program. According to the Centers for Medicare and Medicaid Services (CMS), an accountable care organization (ACO) is "a group of providers and suppliers of services (e.g., hospitals, physicians, and others involved in patient care) that work together to coordinate care for the Medicare Fee-For Service beneficiaries they serve."

As another attempt to reduce cost, the bill will establish a national Medicare pilot program to develop and evaluate paying a bundled payment for acute, inpatient hospital services, physician services, outpatient hospital services, and post-acute care services for an episode of care that begins three days prior to a hospitalization and spans 30 days following discharge.

The bill aims to reduce waste, fraud, and abuse in public programs by allowing provider screening, enhanced oversight periods for new providers and suppliers (including a 90-day period of enhanced oversight for initial claims of some suppliers), and by requiring Medicare and Medicaid program providers and suppliers to establish compliance programs.

The bill also establishes an Independent Payment Advisory Board comprised of 15 members to submit legislative proposals containing recommendations to reduce the per capita rate of growth in Medicare spending if spending exceeds a target growth rate. The Board is prohibited from submitting proposals that would: ration care, increase revenues, or change benefits, eligibility or Medicare beneficiary cost sharing.

Improve Health Care Delivery

To qualify as an ACO, a group of coordinated health care providers must agree to be accountable to the patients and the third-party payor for the quality, appropriateness and efficiency of the health care provided. The idea is that by increasing care coordination, ACOs can help reduce unnecessary medical care and improve health outcomes, leading to a decrease in utilization of acute care services and thereby achieving cost reductions. An ACO must also have adequate participation of primary care physicians, define processes to promote evidence-based medicine, and report on quality of care provided to the community it services.

An ACO is characterized by a care delivery model that ties provider reimbursements to quality metrics and reductions in the total cost of care for its population of patients. The ACO may use a range of payment models (capitation, fee-for-service with shared savings, etc.) to achieve its goals.

Additionally, PPACA will reduce Medicare payments to hospitals to account for preventable hospital readmissions, hospital-acquired conditions and health care acquired conditions.

The bill has authorized the Food and Drug Administration to approve generic versions of biologic agents and to grant pharmaceutical manufacturers only 12 years of exclusive use before generics can be developed.

Another strategy to improve quality is through support of comparative effectiveness research by the not for profit Patient-Centered Outcomes Research Institute (PCORI). PCORI will identify research priorities and conduct research that compares the clinical effectiveness of medical treatments.

PPACA creates an Innovation Center within CMS to test, evaluate, and expand Medicare, Medicaid, and CHIP payment structures and methodologies to reduce program expenditures while maintaining or improving quality of care.

The bill also awards five-year demonstration grants to states to develop, implement, and evaluate alternatives to current tort litigation.

To further improve the longitudinal care of patients, PPACA will create the Independence at Home Demonstration program to provide high-need Medicare beneficiaries with primary care services in their home and allow participating teams of health professionals to share in any savings if they reduce preventable hospitalizations, prevent hospital readmissions, improve health outcomes, improve the efficiency of care, reduce the cost of health care services, and achieve patient satisfaction.

PPACA aims to develop a national quality of care strategy which includes priorities to improve the delivery of health care services, patient health outcomes, and population health. It will create processes for the development of quality measures involving input from multiple stakeholders and for selection of quality measures to be used in reporting to, and payment under, federal health programs.

As part of PPACA, the National Prevention, Health Promotion and Public Health Council will be established to coordinate federal prevention, wellness, and public health activities. The bill will establish a grant program to support the delivery of evidence-based and community-based prevention and wellness services aimed at strengthening prevention activities, reducing chronic disease rates and addressing health disparities, especially in rural and frontier areas.

PPACA includes other details in addition to the aforementioned which relate to tax changes, subsidies to employers, health insurance exchanges, adjustments to payments made by Medicare and Medicaid as well as changes to long-term care financing.

Insurance – Protecting Your Pillars

Insurance products help to protect your income, health, property, and to ensure the continuity of your business. In the *Pillars of Wealth* context, insurance products can be viewed as a sequence of protective domes that shield your pillars against dangers. Each insurance product adds an additional layer of protection against a specific threat. Your personal or household circumstances determine whether and how much insurance you need.

While there are many highly effective uses of insurance, the insurance industry has all too often generated controversy with poorly designed and mispriced products, as well as overly zealous agents pushing unsuitable products. As a consequence, consumers have grown highly suspicious of insurance products and the agents who sell them.

Insurance agents are compensated on the basis of commission. A bigger sale generally means a higher commission, which means you need to be wary that an agent may try to sell you too much insurance, or the wrong product.

Agents are taught that consumers can be influenced most effectively using one of two emotions: fear and greed. Accordingly, insurers and their agents like to bombard us with scary statistics on the prevalence of disabilities, the likelihood of lawsuits, the probability of property damage, as well as morbidity and mortality rates. They also shamelessly seduce us with promises of great financial rewards (e.g., aggressive returns on annuities and variable life insurance policies, as well as tax-free death benefits).

Since insurers have been doing this to hapless consumers for centuries, laws against misrepresentation are quite stringent. But this doesn't stop agents from using unfounded implications when they have us behind closed doors. If in doubt about any assertions made by an agent, take a few minutes to identify the source and confirm what you've been told. Then consider carefully whether you really need the protection in question.

The observation that an insurance agent appears less than 100% sincere doesn't automatically mean you don't need the coverage, but it does mean you should speak with a different agent.

The features and conditions of insurance offerings change over time. Consult a properly licensed insurance agent for the latest details.

What Exactly is Insurance For?

In an earlier chapter we discussed risk in the investing context. We called that *speculative* risk, where we take on the risk voluntarily with a view to receiving some expected reward.

But many risks we face are not voluntary, and they don't offer a reward. We refer to these as *Pure Risks*.

According to Investopedia:

> *Pure risk is a category of risk in which loss is the only possible outcome; there is no beneficial result. Pure risk is related to events that are beyond the risk-taker's control and, therefore, a person cannot consciously take on pure risk.*

So, a pure risk is one in which there's a potential downside or loss, but there's no beneficial upside: the only reward is that the bad outcome has not happened. One example of pure risk is the possibility of being injured or killed in a traffic accident.

Let's compare this to an investment risk such as buying a stock. We buy stock because we want some potential gain or positive return. In contrast, in the traffic accident example we're not consciously making a risk-return tradeoff. There's no distinct upside to travelling on the roads. It's simply something we do as part of life. We have to get to work, go shopping, and pick up our children after school. No one is standing and cheering at each destination, ready to give us some cash for completing our trip successfully.

Similarly, we don't choose exposure to a disabling disease for any upside. We simply accept that risk as an inevitable aspect of life. But we don't have to allow pure risk realizations (such as death, disability, or personal liability) to destroy our household finances and devastate our families. Instead, we can use insurance to mitigate these risks.

So we now have the answer to the question "what is insurance for?" It's for mitigating the pure risks that we have to face but don't get compensated for (in terms of an expected reward).

Mitigation in this context doesn't mean that we *avoid* facing the negative outcome. That is, we can't buy insurance that guarantees we'll never suffer a negative outcome. Rather, the mitigation is in the form of financial support that helps us and our family to weather the consequences of that bad outcome.

So disability insurance doesn't stop you from becoming disabled, but it does replace your income while you're disabled. Life insurance doesn't stop you from dying due to a terminal illness, but it can provide a large sum of money to ensure your spouse and children are taken care of. Malpractice insurance doesn't guarantee you won't be sued for malpractice, but it does provide you with a legal defense team and money to compensate patients in the event a judgment goes against you.

Identifying Good Insurance Companies

If you know nothing about insurance, you likely find the task of identifying a good provider daunting. When it comes to insurance, and in particular life insurance, it's usually advisable to obtain coverage over a long term. In turn, this means we want some assurance that the insurer is going to be around long enough to make good on any claims we (or our beneficiaries) may have. Here are some tips for identifying the better providers:

1. Look for companies that have been in business for a long time. Fifty to a hundred years is a long time
2. Be aware that *mutual* companies have an allegiance to their policyholders (who are also the owners of the mutual company) while *stock* companies have an allegiance to their stockholders (who more than likely are not the same people as the policyholders)

3. Look for insurance companies with the highest independent ratings. Ratings are provided by firms such as A.M. Best, Standard & Poor's, Moody's Investors' Service, and Fitch Ratings. Each rating agency publishes its rating scale. You can find these scales online. Focus on insurance providers with the best ratings (financially the strongest and most creditworthy ones).

Many insurers describe their benefits, or a subset of their benefits as 'guaranteed.' This does not mean benefits are risk-free. It means they are promised—*as long as the insurance company is healthy.* If the company collapses, the guarantees may be invalidated; all the more reason to identify a company with solid long-term prospects.

Insurance is state-specific. There's no federal body regulating insurance companies. Instead, each state has its own insurance Commissioner. While insurance-related laws are similar across most states, California and New York stand out as distinct outliers. Insurance agents often grumble about how much more annoying it is to comply with California and New York insurance rules. This isn't directly your problem, but it's useful to be aware that the differences exist.

Insurance Types

You should consider several types of insurance to protect your household:

1. Disability (short-term and/or long-term; either may be offered by your employer)
2. Property and Casualty (auto, home, motorcycle, boat, recreational vehicle, umbrella)
3. Life (term or permanent; some term coverage may be provided by your employer)
4. Long-Term Care (for yourself or a dependent)
5. Medical Malpractice (may be provided by employer; discussed in previous chapters)
6. Legal Insurance (may be provided through an employer)
7. Health, Dental, Vision (usually provided by employer)

Disability, property & casualty, life, and long-term care insurance are discussed later in this chapter.

Medical malpractice and legal insurance are described in the Employment Contract chapter.

Health/Dental/Vision insurance is almost always provided by your employer. Speak with your human resources representative for coverage details.

Policies offered through an employer may expire when you leave your job. Also, many employer-provided policies are fairly limited, so it can be advisable to supplement them with private insurance. Examples are disability and life insurance. When you obtain your own portable private insurance, you don't lose it when you change jobs (as long as you continue to pay premiums in timely fashion).

Key Features & Terminology

The Premium

Premium is the amount paid by the insured/policyholder to the insurer (the insurance company) for the policy. The premium amount typically depends on the insured's gender, age, state of health, relevant track record (for example, pre-existing medical conditions, prior accidents or speeding tickets) and amount of coverage. Premiums may be paid monthly or annually, and sometimes quarterly or semi-annually. You may be charged extra if you choose not to pay the upfront annual fee all at once each year. If a premium payment is missed, the policy may *lapse*, which can mean losing coverage.

The Benefit

The *benefit* is the amount(s) payable by the insurance company to the insured or a beneficiary when the insured (or policyholder) becomes eligible for payment as a consequence of suffering a financial or property loss, physical injury, disease, or death.

Deductible

The *deductible* is the dollar amount that must be paid by the insured, before the insurer begins to pay benefit(s). Usually, by electing higher deductible amounts you can reduce your premiums. This is because you're accepting more of the risk, and the insurer rewards you for that by reducing your premiums.

Pre-Existing Condition

A *pre-existing condition* is a health or medical issue an applicant has prior to applying for insurance. Many insurers will exclude pre-existing conditions from coverage, or enforce a waiting period before coverage begins. For example, a person with a prior back injury may be able to obtain disability insurance, but the policy may specifically *exclude* (not cover) any spine-related ailments. In some cases, the presence of a pre-existing condition may make the applicant ineligible for coverage or *uninsurable*.

Exclusions from Coverage

Insurers may tailor policies to delay or *exclude* (refuse) coverage for a variety of reasons. Some examples are exclusion due to a specific pre-existing condition such as cancer (in the case of life insurance), flood or earthquake damage (in the case of property insurance), or back/spine coverage (in the case of disability insurance).

Exclusion Period

The *exclusion period* (also known as a pre-existing condition waiting period) is the period of time that an insurer can delay coverage of a pre-existing condition.

Elimination Period

The *elimination period* (or waiting period) is the period of time which must go by after filing a claim and before a policyholder can collect insurance benefits.

Illustration

An insurance *illustration* provides a written summary of premiums, benefits, and other pertinent facts as the proposed policy evolves over time. For example, in a permanent life insurance policy, the illustration may show dividends, cash value, and death benefits for each year the policy is expected to be in force. Some of the items shown on an illustration may depend on assumptions made by the insurance company. It's important to be able to distinguish which of the calculated amounts are guaranteed, and which are non-guaranteed forecasts.

Benefit Period

The *benefit period* is the period of time (in days, months, or years) over which benefits are paid to the policyholder, her dependents, or beneficiaries.

Non-Cancellable and Guaranteed Renewable

Combined, these terms guarantee that as long as you continue to pay your premiums on time, the insurance company cannot cancel your coverage, raise your premiums or change the terms of your policy without your consent. If a policy is only *guaranteed renewable*, as long as you make your payments on time it can't be cancelled and its provisions can't be changed, but premiums can be increased.

Term

The *term* is the period of time over which the policy is in effect. For example, a 10-year Term Life Insurance policy provides coverage for 10 years.

Riders

Riders are additional features or benefits that can be added to a basic insurance policy. While some riders are free, usually riders require additional payment, which increases premiums.

Examples of some riders include:

- *Disability Waiver of Premium* – under some circumstances, life insurance premium payments will be waived if the insured becomes disabled

- *Accidental Death Benefit* – beneficiaries receive additional death benefit if death results from an accident

- *Accelerated Death Benefit* – makes death benefit funds available prior to actual death in cases of terminal illness
- *Guaranteed Purchase Option* – the insured can add more coverage without being medically tested again

Medical Exam

For life and disability policies, insurers will require that you submit to medical testing (blood and urine tests are fairly standard requirements, along with documentation of your health history). If any ailment or condition is discovered during such tests, higher premiums may be required to secure coverage, or you may be deemed uninsurable.

A desirable feature in most policies is the option to increase coverage in future without having to submit to additional medical testing. This is an important consideration and one you should explore in advance with your properly licensed insurance agent.

Insurers will try to get their hands on any bit of information that refines their estimates of your likelihood of becoming disabled or dying prematurely. Genetic test results could be held against you. It may make sense to secure insurance coverage before undertaking genetic testing.

Disability Insurance

There are many diseases and injuries that can cause total or partial disability. To protect against the resulting loss of income, you can purchase *disability insurance* (DI).

DI is particularly important for doctors because they spend a relatively large amount of time and money (not to mention blood, sweat and tears) on becoming medical professionals. Many of them also end up carrying very significant amounts of debt that can only be paid back with reasonably high earnings. Suffering a debilitating injury or disease that precludes you from those earnings can be financially and emotionally devastating. DI helps to protect the very significant investment you've already made in yourself and your career path.

A key consideration when it comes to disability insurance is that if you buy your own insurance and you pay for it with after tax dollars, any benefits you receive may be income-tax free.

Basic Disability Insurance

The most common Disability Insurance is for protecting income. For example, if you're covered by disability insurance and suffer a debilitating injury or disease, you can receive some percentage of your monthly income in benefits. Many group policies (those provided by your employer) will cover up to 50% or 60% of monthly income in case of disability, typically subject to a cap. High earners often need to supplement group policies with additional private insurance to reproduce more of their much higher income.

As your income increases, you typically don't cancel one policy and get a replacement. Rather, you can: (1) purchase a rider (in advance) on your original policy that allows you to increase coverage, or (2) add a new policy to cover the increase in coverage. The new policy layers on top of the existing one. A doctor who is close to retirement may have five or six layers of policies, each incrementally increasing her coverage.

Choosing a *Level* premium option means your premium remains constant throughout the policy's life. In contrast, the *Increasing Rate* option gives you a policy whose premiums are initially relatively low but increase each year. One strategy is to switch from the increasing rate policy to a level one as soon as it becomes affordable to do so.

I recommend purchasing a good policy *at the latest* a year before finishing up residency or fellowship—whichever is the final stage before going on the 'real' job market. Advantages to doing this early are that you can lock-in a lower premium when younger. The likelihood of being rejected from coverage is lower when you're younger and healthier. Getting coverage early usually means lower probability of exclusions, which in turn can mean more favorable (broader) coverage.

Ideally, once approved by a provider, you shouldn't need to undergo medical testing again for additional layers. You should only need to prove that your income has increased. You should confirm this with your agent.

DI premiums depend on many factors, including gender, age, occupation, your state of health, and the fine details of what is and isn't covered. Statistically, women tend to go on disability more than men. Hence, their DI premiums are, on average, higher than those for men of comparable age, health and occupation.

Your employer's group policy typically terminates when employment ends. You should consider obtaining a private *portable* policy that travels with you from employer to employer. Other advantageous policy characteristics include (1) *non-cancellable and guaranteed renewable* (defined earlier in this chapter under the Key Features & Terminology section) and (2) *own occupation*. With a standard disability policy, your benefits usually end when you're healthy enough to rejoin the work force. With an own occupation policy, you may be eligible for continuing disability benefits if you cannot perform your previously specified occupation, and you may still be able to work in some other capacity. This is known in the industry as 'double dipping'—you can earn money through a job and receive disability benefit payments at the same time. A more narrowly defined 'own occupation' is generally more advantageous for you (it may require a higher premium). Take a very close look at the own occupation definition in your policy. Some are more favorable than others.

Think carefully when given the option to obtain lifetime coverage, as such policies will be more expensive than those offering more limited time coverage. Consider all your circumstances fully before making the decision.

In many policies, coverage ends around age 65. You can sometimes get short term policies above this age, but these will be costly because people over age 60 who qualify for disability tend to remain disabled. From the insurer's perspective, older people are not good candidates to insure, so their premiums are very high.

Some insurers will provide discounts when multiple employees of the same company, especially of different ages, apply for insurance. This is simply because signing up multiple employees helps to diversify the insurer's risk and they are willing to pass their savings on to clients.

There are several other types of disability insurance. These are described below.

Student Loans

Some insurers will provide coverage on student loans issued to medical, dental, law, veterinary, or pharmacy students. There's usually a ceiling on the amount covered under these insurance products, often $2,000 per month. In the event of a qualifying disability, the insurer will pay up to the monthly limit directly to the lender.

Depending on the insurance company, student loan coverage may be a standalone policy or one that layers on top of a basic disability policy.

Some student loans are dischargeable in the event of a serious disability, which could obviate the need for this coverage.

Retirement Plan Coverage

When a person becomes *totally* disabled, reduction or termination of monthly income is not the only negative financial outcome. The totally disabled person is no longer contributing to 401(k) or 403(b) accounts, and is also likely no longer eligible to receive matching contributions from his employer. Retirement plan coverage insurance can provide up to several thousand dollars (a maximum of around $4,000) per month to make up for lost contributions to 401(k), 403(b), and potentially other retirement accounts.

If you own a private practice, there are other policies you could consider, including: business overhead expense, business loan coverage, and disability buy-out. These policies are discussed in the second *Pillars of Wealth* book: *Finance & Business Essentials for Medical Practices*.

Property and Casualty Insurance

Damage to, and liability associated with, your home, auto, boat, plane, or motorcycle may be covered through *Property and Casualty insurance*.

Property insurance is designed to protect against damage or loss to property such as a home, vehicle, or business. Coverage usually extends to instances of theft, collision, fire, and some weather damage. Protection against floods and earthquakes must often be purchased separately.

Casualty (or *liability*) insurance covers an individual (or a business) in cases where negligence or an act of omission causes injury to another person. For example, automobile insurance may provide liability coverage in the event a driver is deemed to have been responsible for an accident. Coverage may extend to the medical expenses of victims, repair of their property, as well as their lost wages and potentially any other loss or damage they can establish.

Standard homeowner and automobile policies may limit liability coverage to an amount in the range of $200,000 to $300,000. Clearly, a serious accident can lead to much higher liability. The upshot is that you may be personally liable for any excess above the covered limit. It's therefore highly advisable to extend liability coverage through the use of a Personal Umbrella or Personal Catastrophe Liability (PCL) insurance policy. Such policies tend to be relatively affordable. I highly recommend that you consider purchasing at least $2 million of such coverage. Consult with your insurance specialist in order to determine the coverage level that is appropriate for your circumstances.

Given the litigious nature of American society, you should avoid publicly discussing your liability limits, as this could affect the likelihood that someone will sue you, and the size of any lawsuit.

Life Insurance

Life Insurance protects beneficiaries against loss of income due to the death of the insured. Life insurance is one of the most complex and confusing areas of financial planning. It's also one of the more important areas, because not having appropriate insurance in the event of a tragic death can be financially devastating for a household.

On average, women have higher life expectancy than men. For this reason women generally pay lower life insurance premiums (for the same coverage) than men of comparable age and health.

One of the first big questions when it comes to life insurance is: *how much do I need?* Below we discuss two common calculation methods: human life value and financial need.

Human Life Value

Human life value is based on the insured's projected future income. As a rough estimate, take the number of years a person has left until retirement and multiply that by the annual income that person can expect to receive over those years. The product is the person's human life value—the total economic value that person's labor is expected to produce.

Incorporation of time value of money and other adjustments can provide a more refined estimate. Human life value is commonly applied in legal cases.

Financial Need

Financial Need is estimated by calculating the financial needs of the surviving family or dependents the (deceased) insured leaves behind. Counting up the outstanding liabilities of the household (e.g., mortgage, student loans, and car payments) along with estimated amounts for spouse and children's food, clothing, education, medical care needs, etc., one can estimate the total dollar amount needed to take care of those left behind. The estimates can reflect coverage that lasts until those dependants can: (1) fend for themselves (in the case of children) or (2) live with dignity through retirement (in the case of spouse or other older dependents).

Insurance agents have the incentive to recommend that you buy more rather than less insurance, so they may emphasize the valuation method that yields the higher number. Using the human life value approach it's easy to reach numbers in excess of $10 million dollars, but few families really need that level of coverage. It may be flattering to think we are 'worth' $10 to $20 million, but in reality insuring yourself to such a level may be unnecessarily expensive. Once you accept an expensive policy, you're obligated to continue making those high payments according to the policy terms. This obligation could become a serious burden later on.

There are two types of life insurance: term and permanent.

Term Insurance

Term Insurance provides coverage in the event of the insured's death, but coverage applies only over a specified period of time or

Term. Typical terms are ten, twenty, and thirty years. Term insurance tends to be quite affordable, but this depends on your state of health at time of application. A healthy person in her early thirties could pay less than $500 per year for a twenty-year, $1 million death benefit policy. The downside with these policies is that once they expire, the coverage disappears. So if you die a day after coverage expires, your beneficiaries get nothing!

If you opt for a twenty-year term policy when you are thirty years old, it will expire when you are fifty years old. At that point if you want to obtain coverage you'll have to undergo medical testing again. Your annual premiums at age fifty will be dramatically higher than your initial policy premiums.

The worst case scenario may be that you will be deemed uninsurable after being tested again, leaving you without any protection. It's important to think ahead when you purchase coverage. Opting for a thirty-year term policy at age thirty will get you covered until age sixty. If you make good financial decisions over those thirty years, you may have your home paid off, all children may have completed college, and you and your spouse may have a tidy nest egg for retirement. At that point you may no longer care whether you're insurable because you may not need the insurance.

Some term insurance is *convertible*. This means it can be converted at some future date to a permanent life insurance policy. This can be useful if you have interest in one or more of the permanent policy features. A common reason to make the conversion is to accumulate cash value (described below). The key is to ensure that the conversion is possible without having to be medically tested again.

Permanent Insurance

Permanent insurance remains in force as long as you continue to pay your premiums. Thus, properly maintained permanent insurance *will* pay death benefits when you die. (In contrast, statistically speaking, the vast majority of term policies don't end in death benefit payments as most people outlive their term limits). Coupled with the ability to accumulate cash value in a permanent policy, these two features explain why *for a given death benefit amount*, permanent insurance costs much more than term insurance.

Insurance agents often use a *renting vs. buying a home analogy* here. The purchase of term insurance is equivalent to 'renting' insurance coverage for a limited period of time, whereas purchasing of permanent insurance is 'buying' coverage for your lifetime. In the case of the latter, you are 'building up equity' in the policy in the form of cash value. The analogy is repeated here to help explain the differences. It's not meant to encourage you to rush out and buy a permanent policy.

The main features of permanent life insurance usually include:

- Some fraction of each of your premium payments is saved or invested on your behalf. Thus, over time, you're creating cash value or in our context, a pillar of wealth

- You may be eligible for dividends. Insurers usually make an effort to offer a fairly stable stream of dividend payments. But such payments are not guaranteed

- Cash value accumulates tax deferred—you don't have to pay taxes on the investment gains in the policy cash value—unless and until you elect to withdraw them

- You can surrender the policy for its cash value, pay off the relevant taxes, and keep the rest

- There's an alternative way to access your cash value without surrendering the policy. You simply borrow against the cash value. That is, you take out a loan from the insurance company against the cash value you've accumulated. It should be possible to borrow this money without triggering taxes, but you have to pay interest to the insurance company on those loans. And the amount lent to you is no longer accumulating interest in the cash value account. Taking out a loan can seriously throw off your illustrated returns

- You may be able to add riders to your policy. Some examples include: (1) Disability Income Rider providing you with monthly payments to replace your income in the event of disability, and (2) Acceleration of Death Benefit Rider allowing you to receive some cash prior to death in the event of a terminal illness diagnosis. You usually have to pay for riders. Some are touted as free but insurers don't really give anything of value away. Be wary of these added features as they may not be worth the cost

In many policies (especially Whole Life) it may take a decade or more to accumulate a meaningful amount of cash value. If you expect to use the cash in the near term, it's probably best to avoid a permanent policy.

Reduced Paid-Up Policy

A permanent life insurance policy may be convertible into a fully *paid-up* policy (i.e., no more premiums need to be paid) with a lower payout (lower death benefit). Generally, this is only possible after an extended period of time, during which the cash value of the policy has grown sufficiently. That cash value is used to buy a fully paid-up policy.

There are several categories of permanent insurance, including Whole Life, Universal Life, and Variable Life. Some of these have their own variants (e.g., Indexed Universal Life, Variable Universal Life, No-Lapse Universal Life, etc.)

Whole Life Insurance

Whole Life (WL) policies are generally characterized by guarantees and stability. Your premiums are fixed (they don't change over time), you're guaranteed a minimum death benefit, and a minimum rate of return on your cash value in the form of interest paid by the insurer. In addition to the guaranteed interest rate, you may receive dividends. Retaining the dividends within the policy provides an opportunity for greater cash value growth and enhanced death benefit.

Due to the guarantees in a Whole Life policy, the premiums are large. This also means that commissions are hefty and hence very appealing to the agents who sell them. This raises the question of whether a policy is being sold for the right reasons: true needs of the consumer or to enrich the agent. I address such issues later.

The very rigid terms of WL policies can become a constraint for the policy owner. Cash value takes a long time to build, and large premiums must be paid consistently—over decades. To keep the policy in force until death, the owner must pay premiums until death.

Furthermore, as a fixed income instrument, the cash value of a whole life policy can be undermined in a highly inflationary environment.

Universal Life Insurance

Unlike Whole Life's fixed premiums, *Universal Life* (UL) policies offer adjustable premiums. This means you can elect to pay more into the policy when you have extra cash, or to pay less when cash is scarce. There's also greater flexibility in increasing or decreasing the death benefit.

Some Universal Life policies allow you to choose between guaranteed cash value returns (you likely will not be eligible for dividends) or indexing returns to stock market performance (Indexed Universal Life or IUL). You can usually switch back and forth between these alternatives at least once a year.

Downsides are that a Universal policy may lapse under certain conditions, including: changes in the insurer's mortality assumptions, increases in administrative expenses, underperformance of the underlying investment portfolio, or insufficient premium payments.

Cash value depends on the performance of underlying investments. In the event these investments perform poorly, cash value accumulation may be disappointing.

Due to the flexibility of Universal Life policies, they are often used in estate planning.

Variable Life Insurance

Variable Life (VL) policies allow a broader variety of investment options. Unlike the conservative nature of Whole Life investments (primarily in high quality bonds), variable life premiums may be invested in a wide range of securities, often stock and bond funds. These funds exhibit a wide range of risk and return characteristics.

Insurance companies began to offer variable policies in an effort to compete with stock market returns. Consumers increasingly questioned the point of purchasing relatively low-return Whole Life policies when they thought they could double their returns by investing in stock markets.

Insurers wanted to attract these consumers, but they didn't want to have to guarantee higher returns, so they created the glamorous seeming VL product and touted its market return potential. The downside was (and remains) that consumers shoulder all the investment risk.

With Whole Life policies, your cash value is invested in the insurer's General Account, and the insurer is responsible for managing those investments on your behalf. The insurer guarantees you some minimal performance through fixed promised interest rates (and usually fairly stable dividends). In contrast, Variable Life contributions are managed in a Separate Account. You get to choose the underlying investments, and you may be able to change them over time. But as noted above, you bear full responsibility for the investment performance.

To sell Variable Life policies, an agent must have an insurance license *and* a securities license.

Variable Universal Life (VUL) allows you: to choose from a broad set of risky investment alternatives *and* flexibility to alter your premiums.

Whole Life is positioned on the most conservative end of the permanent policy spectrum, while Variable Life is at the opposite— most speculative end. Universal Life tends to be positioned between these two extremes.

Permanent policies are complex instruments with lots of moving parts. Each insurer has its own preferred bells and whistles. This makes it very difficult to create true apples-to-apples comparisons.

The Term vs. Permanent Debate

One of the most ubiquitous financial planning one-liners is "Buy Term—Invest the Difference." The implication is that instead of buying 'expensive' permanent insurance, you should buy term coverage for less money, and place the excess in investments such as stocks. In the interest of brevity, I'll call this the BTID strategy.

I have two reasons for highlighting BTID. The first is that the approach is generally the right outcome for many households. The second is that just because it is *often* the better choice, doesn't mean it is *always* the better choice. This observation was made earlier in the decision making section of this book—our tendency to resort to reflexive one-liners and blanket statements. Instead we should acknowledge potential subtleties by beginning our answers with 'it depends…'

Fans of the BTID strategy often perform calculations and then declare (predictably) that buying term and investing the rest yields a higher expected return.

Why is this a predictable result?

Because a typical Whole Life permanent policy may offer 4% interest plus dividends on the order of around 1-2% (for a total of around 5-6%). From this you have to subtract various expenses to arrive at an annual return, so the highest return you could aspire to would probably be under 5%. Stock investments are assumed to yield around 8-10% annually. Thus, it's inevitable that BTID will look better in such comparisons.

As already noted, for many consumers a good term policy is a solid, and arguably a better, choice than Whole Life. But in the interest of intellectual honesty, you should be aware that these comparisons are often flawed. The very notion of comparing term and permanent policies misses the point. They're not two versions of the same product, differing only on price. They're different products offering a different set of benefits. In fact, they're comparable in only one way: both provide a death benefit in the event the insured dies. In every other way, they're different.

To emphasize these differences I like to use a pharmaceutical analogy: Suppose a patient is susceptible to five ailments. As a physician you can prescribe 5 separate pills, which have efficacy rates ranging from 80-100% per ailment. This requires the patient to take five separate treatments, with all associated inconvenience and cost. Instead, suppose you could prescribe a single combination pill that addresses all five ailments, with efficacy rates of 70-80% per ailment, and in at least one case, 100%.

Let's take this to the financial context, where the five 'Ailments' are the following financial dangers:

1. Survivors' financial exposure in event breadwinner dies
2. Need for emergency cash to cover urgent expense(s)
3. Running out of money in retirement
4. High taxes severely undermining nest egg growth
5. Creditor lawsuits threatening to take pillars

Each of these has its own individual or standalone remedy (downsides are noted in parentheses):

1) The individual remedy is to purchase term life insurance. Term insurance costs less than permanent insurance. (There is the

downside of outliving the term policy and ending up without any coverage thereafter)

2) The individual remedy is to use a credit card or obtain a bank loan. (The downside in such cases is that credit card loans have high interest rates, and it may take too long to qualify for a bank loan)

3) The individual remedy is to start saving early and invest in financial securities offering growth and income. (The downside is that markets may turn against you, leading to deep losses)

4) The individual remedy is investment in tax-deferred vehicles such as IRA, 401(k), or 403(b) accounts. (The downsides are that there are: limits to how much you can put into tax-qualified accounts, stringent rules, and penalties for early withdrawals or failure to take distributions after retirement)

5) The individual remedy is to put your money into protected assets—those that are outside the reach of creditors. For example, in some states a family's primary home has such protection. An alternative response is to hope and pray that no one will ever sue you—the risk management equivalent of an ostrich sticking its head in the ground. (The downsides are that while scrambling to protect assets, you may deprive your family or yourself of access to those assets or expose yourself to unfavorable tax implications)

A permanent Whole Life insurance policy is analogous to the combination pill, as it offers all of the following simultaneously:

1. Death benefit protection addressing Ailment 1 (100% efficacy as long as premiums are paid)
2. Loan provision addressing Ailment 2 (contingent on building up sufficient cash value)
3. Cash value accumulation option (partly) addressing Ailment 3
4. Tax deferral and income-tax free death benefit for beneficiaries addressing Ailment 4
5. Protection against lawsuits and creditors addressing Ailment 5 (depending on state law)

Those in favor of the BTID strategy effectively focus on item 3, arguing that they can build up much larger amounts of cash by investing directly in stock markets.

Yes, direct investment in stocks and bonds—the individual treatment of Ailment 3—*may* lead to higher average returns over extended periods than the average growth in cash value of a permanent insurance policy, but there's no guarantee of this.

It's easy to criticize any one feature of the combo pill. But the point is that the combo pill is much more than any one feature. It's all of them combined. Just because one feature of the combo treatment doesn't look as favorable as some other focused treatment, doesn't invalidate all the other benefits of the combo treatment. They are still there, ready whenever the need arises. If you know with certainty that you'll never need those other features (and you are willing to take the downside risk—such as outliving your term insurance and dying a day after it expires), then by all means, you should go with individual treatment(s). If, on the other hand, you see value and convenience in the combination treatment, permanent insurance may be appropriate for you and your family.

From a financial engineering perspective, one could say that the multiple features of permanent life insurance provide options for the policyholder, and each option has a value. Thus, focusing on just one feature is effectively ignoring the option values of all other features. Can you be sure that you won't need these options in future?

At the very least, taking these option values into account makes the permanent option *less unfavorable*. The permanent policy tends to appear even more appealing if you've already maxed out all your usual tax-deferral vehicles, are in a high tax bracket, and feel a need for some asset protection. With each of these arguments the reflexive BTID strategy seems less convincing.

Let's take on the main assumption utilized by the BTID camp: it relies almost exclusively on the idea that stock market returns won't let us down in future. It's taken as gospel that markets will continue to offer average returns on the order of 8-10% annually.

As a risk management expert I've been trained to suggest the unthinkable: *what if those historical averages don't hold up over the next twenty to thirty years? Are there reasonable scenarios under which we'll be seeing lower returns? Is there some divine edict that guarantees us such returns?* Any responsible individual should acknowledge that there are no such guarantees. Furthermore, I've already provided a legitimate argument for why future American stock returns may not be as high as they have been in the past (Please refer to the section "Some Thoughts on American Stock Market Returns" in the Investing Basics & Account Types chapter).

Recognition that lower future market returns are possible stabs deeply into the heart of the BTID camp.

To be clear, I'm not urging you to run out and buy permanent life insurance. I'm using this as a case study where the *Eureka* moment is the realization that subtle details are very important. Sure, it's easier to wrap ourselves in blanket statements, but it's not necessarily correct to do so.

If you do want lifetime coverage but you have no interest (or faith) in the cash value accumulation of typical permanent insurance, you can opt for a Guaranteed No-Lapse UL policy. This is a policy that can be in effect for your lifetime at a much lower premium than a Whole Life policy. The lower premium is possible because such policies don't offer any meaningful cash value accumulation.

With typical UL policies, if cash value dwindles to zero, the policy may lapse, or expire. The aforementioned no-lapse guarantee ensures the policy will not self-destruct. But even such 'guarantees' are vulnerable. For example, in some cases missing one premium payment by a single day could invalidate the no-lapse guarantee. As noted earlier, guarantees may also not mean much if the insurer runs into financial difficulties.

General Criticisms of Permanent Policies

Permanent life insurance policies have been heavily criticized over the years. Much of this criticism is well founded:

1. High commissions motivate agents to push permanent policies aggressively
2. Policies may not yield promised cash values and long–term returns
3. Policies may self-destruct due to reasons that are hidden in small print
4. Unnecessary bells and whistles pushed by shady agents cost more than they are worth

So you must be *very* careful before committing to such policies.

I'm not a cheerleader for the insurance industry, but in the interest of intellectual honesty, I'm compelled to point out that several reflexive criticisms of permanent life insurance products are not completely accurate.

Here are some of my observations:

1. Despite assertions to the contrary, the cash value of permanent life insurance policies *is* an asset. I don't, however, consider permanent insurance to be an asset class. Agents may position it as an asset class in an effort to convince you it's a necessary component of your overall nest egg. It isn't!
2. The cash value of permanent life insurance *can* be considered a Pillar of Wealth, although your particular circumstances determine whether it's a pillar you should own
3. Permanent life insurance *can* provide some diversification to a household's portfolio. This is more of a mathematical assertion. As long as the cash value asset is not perfectly correlated with any other assets the household owns, it does provide some diversification. Having said that, it is legitimate to question how much diversification benefit is provided and whether that justifies holding such an asset. That, of course, depends on specific circumstances

Understandably, reflexive generalizations often come from people who have been burned by insurance products and/or agents. While our anger is justified, it's still important to remain intellectually honest.

Why? Because the general concept of permanent insurance is actually quite reasonable. Our concerns stem primarily from: lack of transparency, excessive commissions and other hidden costs, and our annoyance at being pursued by shady agents. A world in which these concerns are addressed is one in which fairly priced permanent insurance could be useful for more households.

A Brighter Future for Permanent Insurance Policies?

There are some encouraging signs. Insurance companies are increasingly aware of our concerns, and they have some of their own. It's costly for them to maintain large agent networks. And agent ineptitude and dishonesty cause them liability and reputational issues.

The Internet Age may provide relief for both consumers and insurers by ushering in an era of direct-sold policies. By selling standardized policies (online) directly to consumers, insurers will be able to say goodbye to large and expensive agent networks, and to offer simpler, cheaper policies. Consumers will benefit from lower-priced, standardized, more transparent policies, and from not having to deal with commission-based agents.

When this change happens, and there's increasingly reason to believe it will, we should be ready to consider such tools rather than being reflexively biased against them.

Variable Insurance Products

Insurance products such as variable life and variable annuities are pitched to consumers who desire investments with higher returns. But such products require consumers to take on more risk. This defeats the purpose of insurance, which is to reduce risk and uncertainty. The whole point of insurance is that you pay for the peace of mind of taking risk off the table. Why on earth would you purposely obfuscate the situation by creating more uncertainty (in this case through a layer of speculative investing risk)?

At a very basic level, using insurance products as investments doesn't make sense, because they tend to involve too many middle-men and too many fees. The fees undermine returns, making them inferior investments.

If variable products magnify policyholder risks and offer inferior (after-fee) returns, they can't be an efficient investment choice.

Accordingly, I recommend that you stay away from variable products. I can't think of any compelling reason for such products to be offered to the retail public—certainly not in their current opaque, high-fee formats. If you want to chase risky returns, you can do so more efficiently through investment accounts rather than from the inside of insurance policies or annuity contracts.

Long-Term Care Insurance

Long-Term Care insurance (LTC) pays for assistance in the event a person cannot perform certain activities of daily living due to disability, illness or cognitive impairment. The assistance may come in the form of respite care, hospice care, assisted living, Alzheimer's facilities, nursing and home health care, as well as adult day care. Disability is typically defined as inability to perform two or more of the following activities of daily living: dressing, bathing, eating, toileting, continence, and transferring (standing up, walking, sitting down). A formal medical diagnosis from a physician is required to establish disability.

Over the years, a number of concerns have been expressed regarding LTC insurance.

These include:

1. Insurers and brokers overstating the *probability* that LTC insurance will be needed and the *amount* of insurance needed
2. Policies not covering all expenditures
3. Policies not compensating for cost of living adjustments
4. Insurers having the right to raise premiums, forcing clients to pay more or lose coverage

Many people don't need LTC insurance. They fall into two categories. The first consists of those with negligible assets who qualify for long-term care services through Medicaid. The second consists of those with significant assets (at least several hundred thousand dollars in addition to owning their own home), who can afford to pay for long-term care costs directly instead of buying LTC insurance.

This leaves a population of people who have too much in the way of assets to qualify for Medicaid, but realistically, not enough to fund their own anticipated needs. Arguably, this is the population most in need of long-term care insurance, but also a population which may find it difficult to afford the premium payments.

Those who don't have LTC insurance sometimes draw down their assets over several years, and become eligible for Medicaid once their assets decline below the eligibility threshold.

Ultimately, purchase of long-term care insurance for yourself or for your parents depends on your family's specific circumstances and preferences. Consider engaging all stakeholders in a conversation about the available choices. Stakeholders include the prospective patient(s), family members who may provide care, adult children, and spouses. Topics for discussion include whether you prefer to receive care at home or in some other facility; roles of family members, aides or nurses; and how to pay for long-term care expenses (savings, insurance, Medicaid).

Final Thoughts on Insurance

Some older consumers look back and say, "I paid for life insurance and disability insurance and property and casualty insurance for decades. I never used any of it. It was all a waste of money."

You may not use all of the insurance purchased in your lifetime, but since you don't know in advance whether any will be needed, and since the downside can be devastating to your business or family, it's highly advisable to obtain appropriate coverage. The alternative, should disaster strike, is that one or more of your Pillars of Wealth may be severely compromised, leaving you or your loved ones exposed.

Working With a Financial Advisor

Ideally, financial advisors serve as architects and masons who help to design and build our Pillars of Wealth. But in reality, some financial advisors act more like parasites who attach themselves to our pillars and steadily extract wealth for their own use.

This gap between ideal and real is the crux of the problem in the retail financial services industry.

To be sure, there are advisors who provide good service at a fair price. The challenge for you is to distinguish the good—from the bad and the ugly.

My opinion is that the entire retail financial services industry should be scrapped and a new system implemented. In this new system the vast and confusing selection of products would be replaced with a smaller number of simple, standardized, and transparent offerings. Such a radical change would likely put two thirds (or more) of the current providers of retail services out of business. And that, of course, is why the industry has fought tooth and nail to resist change.

Despite this heated opposition, some consumer protections have increased following passage of the Dodd Frank Act (2010) and creation of the Consumer Financial Protection Bureau (CFPB, 2011). But progress has been slow, and behind the scenes, industry lobbyists continuously seek to undermine these protections.

A good first step for you is to gain more knowledge so you can make better decisions and reduce your reliance on unscrupulous or inept advisors. Ultimately, of course, you must decide whether to make all decisions on your own (the Do-It-Yourself path, DIY) or outsource some of them to others. Both paths are legitimate and each has its pros and cons.

DIY versus Using an Advisor

The do-it-yourself (DIY) path is appealing for a variety of reasons:

- You retain full control
- You avoid some risk of fraud
- You avoid exposure to advisor ineptitude
- You may avoid some advisory fees

The downsides of the DIY path are that:

- You don't have a seasoned advisor's expertise available at every key point in your personal and professional life
- You don't have a built-in mechanism for periodic reviews and analysis of your family's evolving financial needs
- You may be prone to more emotion-driven errors (which can cost you a lot of money in the long-run)
- You may find yourself re-inventing the wheel—having to learn many lessons on your own (the hard way)
- You may have less time for family, hobbies, or business

Deciding whether to DIY or work with an advisor hinges on three considerations:

1. Do you have the *knowledge* to consistently make good decisions on your own?
2. Do you have the *time* to spend on the research and analysis required to make good decisions?
3. Do you have the *inclination* to spend time on analysis and decisions?

If the answer to any of these is 'no' then you should consider working with an advisor. Making decisions on your own without knowledge of the underlying facts is like an illiterate patient self-medicating. Good decisions require expertise. If you don't have that expertise, find someone who does.

If you want to make all financial decisions on your own, or have a spouse who is qualified to do so, that's great. Just make sure that within your household, you truly have the required: expertise, time and inclination. I know physicians whose spouses are business owners and/or have MBA degrees, who still decide to seek external advice from qualified financial advisors. Often, that's a very constructive decision. The challenge, of course, is to find someone you trust to consistently provide unbiased advice.

Many doctors already have a trusted advisor, often an accountant or a lawyer. It's comforting to have such relationships. But an attorney is a legal expert and an accountant a tax expert. The accountant and lawyer may be your best friends; they may be fully committed to your well-being. But the bottom line is that neither is likely to be an expert in financial planning or wealth management. If you're not going to do this yourself, find an expert on whom you can rely.

The Basic Functions of Financial Advisors

In order to select a financial advisor, we first need to understand the different functions advisors perform. Individuals or companies we loosely refer to as 'advisors' fulfill the following basic functions:

Investment Advisors

Investment advisors provide investment advice to clients. Based on indicators such as a client's age, income, and risk preferences, they recommend purchases of financial products such as stocks, bonds, mutual funds and other investment alternatives.

Insurance Agents

Insurance agents sell insurance products, including: property and casualty, life, disability, long-term care, and health insurance. They may also sell annuities.

Brokers

Brokers execute financial transactions on behalf of clients. They typically buy and sell stocks and bonds based on client instructions.

Asset Managers

Asset managers construct and maintain portfolios. These portfolios (or funds) are then made available to investors as investment choices.

Financial Planners

Financial planners take a comprehensive view of the client's financial situation and develop a plan meant to achieve the client's intended overall objectives.

Historically, advisors adhered to these designated functions in mutually exclusive fashion: an investment advisor gave advice; an insurance agent sold insurance products; a broker executed trades; an asset manager managed funds; and a financial planner provided a plan. Over recent decades, however, the lines of distinction have blurred significantly.

Some examples of this blurring:

- Brokers once executed trades, but many now also provide advice about investment choices. Some insurance agents are also licensed as brokers, allowing them to sell products such as variable annuities and variable life insurance policies. Brokers may now refer to themselves as financial consultants, financial advisors or investment consultants

- Investment Advisors may suggest proprietary investment vehicles offered by their employers. Or, they may recommend individual investments or portfolios (such as mutual funds) offered by third parties. Investment advisors often refer to themselves as investment managers, asset managers, portfolio managers, and wealth managers

- Financial planners may provide a strategic plan, but may also be licensed to execute any elements of that plan, encompassing: debt management, investments, insurance products, college education, retirement, estate, and tax planning. Financial planners may come from any background, including brokerage, investment advisory, accounting or insurance services.

Often, advice from these professionals skews in favor of their initial training (comfort zone) or their employers' primary industry. Thus, an insurance agent who holds himself out as a financial planner may lean more heavily on insurance products when recommending a financial plan to a client. A broker claiming to provide general investment advice may recommend a complex target portfolio requiring numerous transactions.

It helps if you know exactly which function(s) you need filled, allowing you to focus on finding an unbiased advisor who has appropriate expertise.

The Fundamental Characteristics of Advisors

When evaluating an advisor, always consider several fundamental characteristics: alignment with client interests, fees charged, and professional expertise.

I. Advisor Alignment

Alignment refers to the extent to which the advisor's interests or motives agree with the client's. There are two alignment paradigms:

1. Some advisors have a *fiduciary duty* to you, which means they're legally required to put your interests first, even at their own expense. This is the strongest form of allegiance and the most desirable from your perspective. For example, doctors and lawyers owe their patients and clients a fiduciary duty

2. Other advisors are only required to provide advice that is deemed *suitable* for you and your circumstances. Suitable investments are those that are consistent with your investing objectives, comfort level with risk taking, financial means and age. (For example, investing a 90-year-old widow's entire nest egg in very risky hi-tech stocks would be unsuitable). There's no requirement that suitable recommendations be *best* suited to you, and no obligation to look out for your best interests

Registered Investment Advisors (RIAs) are registered with the U.S. Securities and Exchange Commission (SEC), a federal government body. These advisors generally have a fiduciary duty to their clients—the highest form of allegiance. The same applies to advisors working for smaller, state-registered investment advisory firms.

Some private sector (non-government) credentials also impose a fiduciary duty on advisors. For example, members of the National Association of Personal Financial Advisors (NAPFA) take a fiduciary oath. Those who qualify as Certified Financial Planners™ (CFP®) through the Certified Financial Planner Board of Standards also accept a fiduciary duty when engaged in financial planning.

In contrast, brokers don't have a fiduciary duty. They are bound only by the suitability requirement. Their governing body is the Financial Industry Regulatory Authority (FINRA). Similarly, insurance agents have a suitability obligation but not a fiduciary duty.

The suitability requirement is susceptible to conflicts of interest. A non-fiduciary can legally give you advice that is best for him (it may allow him to earn high fees), but not the best for you.

Advisors who are directly employed by an insurance company, or a firm that provides brokerage services, or one that offers its own (proprietary) investment products, may be conflicted. This is because such advisors most likely have specific financial incentives to sell their employers' products. This means less choice for you, both in terms of product quality and fees. We'll revisit this in the section on Advisor Fees.

Independent Advisors

If you want an advisor who owes you the greatest allegiance and must provide you with the best advice for your situation and circumstances, your logical choice is to utilize the services of an *independent* advisor acting as a fiduciary. Independent advisors are not directly employed by providers of financial products. This means they are free to offer you a broad range of products and services, and to help you make good selections among the various choices.

If you only need help executing trades, a (non-fiduciary) broker may be sufficient. In such cases, consider using a discount brokerage firm that doesn't make trade recommendations and will execute trades at lower fees.

In the wake of the Great Recession some momentum was created to expand fiduciary duty to more financial professionals. After much wrangling, the most recent rules (released in 2016) impose a fiduciary duty on those providing retirement planning advice. This is a partial victory for those seeking greater accountability by providers of financial advice. It means that fiduciary responsibility will apply in more cases than before. But it falls short of requiring all providers of financial services to adhere to a fiduciary duty at all times.

The alignment picture can get quite confusing because legally an advisor may be held to a fiduciary standard when giving you retirement investment advice for your 401(k) account, and later in that same conversation she may be held only to a suitability standard when recommending insurance purchases.

No sane consumer would design a financial services industry that is littered with such confusion. But that's the system we must live with today. It's the result of intense lobbying over decades by industry insiders who have in aggregate extracted billions of dollars in compensation—from our nest eggs! Since the government has not seen fit to provide us with full protection, it falls to us to look out for our own interests. (That is, in a nutshell, the motivation for writing this book).

II. Advisor Fees

Advisors may be compensated in one of several ways:

1. Annually, as a percentage of total assets you (the client) entrust to them (this compensation is referred to as a percentage of assets under management, or AUM)
2. By commissions, payable on each executed transaction
3. By the hour, the same way an attorney would charge
4. With a one-time, all-encompassing fee that is agreed upfront, before services are rendered

Many consumer activists feel that to be truly objective, advisors should be 'fee-only,' which means they don't accept commissions or any external (third party) compensation. In other words, you should be their only source of income. They may charge you a single all-inclusive annual AUM fee, or by the hour, or with a one-time all-in fee.

The other compensation types are considered more susceptible to abuse. For example, a person compensated on a commission basis (acting as a broker) may recommend unnecessary transactions to earn multiple commissions. Or, an advisor may urge clients to buy only those mutual fund investments that make the advisor eligible to receive payment from the mutual fund company. This is an example of the advisor not being paid directly by you, the client. Instead, some advisors are paid their commissions or fees partly or fully by the firms whose products they sell. These costs are often passed on to you, however. More to the point, such compensation mechanisms may create conflicts for the advisor, who benefits from recommending products that are not the best choices for you.

In addition to the 'fee-only' and 'commission' compensation mechanisms, there is the 'fee-based' category. Fee-based (which sounds confusingly similar to fee-only) usually means compensation is a combination of AUM fees and commissions.

AUM fees can be appropriate as long as they're not excessive, and the client receives good value for the fees paid. This begs the questions: What is *value* and how do we define *excessive* fees?

Value

The most objective measure of value is the actual return or growth of your nest egg over time. An advisor who guides you to solid returns or gains is helping you meet your financial goals.

An advisor can also add value by providing a comprehensive strategy within which consistent decisions are made. The alternative, (which unfortunately applies to many doctors), is making a series of inconsistent and inefficient *ad hoc* decisions.

Value may also come in the form of handholding. Advisors are aware that clients often need them to act as psychologists or therapists, especially when markets are volatile or the clients are going through emotional upheaval at home or at work.

Clients also appreciate advisors who can serve as sounding boards, and are accessible on short notice to answer questions and help guide decisions.

Excessive Fees

So what are excessive fees?

This is a somewhat subjective issue, since as noted above, an advisor can add value that isn't directly observable in terms of annual return. Only you can decide whether an advisor's fees are justifiable by his value-added.

In my opinion, even allowing for various forms of value-addition, the typical advisor cannot justify charging average annual fees in excess of 1% of AUM. So as a rule of thumb anything above 1% is your unequivocal signal to run for the hills.

But that doesn't mean that a fee of 0.9% is okay. In the time value of money section we learned that even a small annual fee over 30 years can devastate your next egg. Anything close to 1% will do a lot of damage. So the bottom line is that you want your fees to be as low as possible.

You can probably manage your own investments within a 0.3% to 0.4% range annually if you opt for passive index funds. Some robo-investor firms (those that use computer algorithms to manage your assets) will charge fees in this range. Your average annual fees could be even lower if you use the lowest cost ETFs (those that charge annual fees of 0.1% or even less).

The fees you pay have a huge impact on your long-term prosperity. *You must zealously and continuously act to reduce these fees.* Any advisor who fails to acknowledge this imperative represents a danger to your financial success.

Hidden Perks & Conflicts

We know advisors may be compensated in ways that create serious conflicts. An obvious example is the broker who tries to get you to constantly buy and sell stocks, thereby generating multiple commissions.

But there are other practices that are even more disturbing. Advisors may win cruises or all-expense paid trips to exotic locations by meeting sales goals. For example, consider insurance agents employed directly by insurance companies. Many of these agents are allowed to sell products offered by rival insurance companies. Offering alternatives makes an agent seem more credible. It's easy for him to say that his job is to help you find the best products, even if they're not his employer's products.

What the agent conveniently doesn't say is that if he generates some threshold (say $100,000) in commissions from his *own* employer's products, he gets an extra cash bonus or is eligible to go on a free cruise with his spouse. He may also receive a ring or a gold watch denoting that he's a member of some elite circle of salespeople within his firm. There are also industry-wide awards for agents who meet certain productivity goals. Such highly coveted distinctions are prestigious within the industry and give agents bragging rights. These perks persist because historically they've proven to be highly effective in motivating competitive salespeople.

All this boils down to the agent insisting that you're being presented with an objective selection of competitive products, while secretly having every incentive to subtly steer you to those products that add to his cruise-eligible sales.

Where do you think the money comes from to pay for his cruise and diamond ring or gold watch? The insurance company will tell you that it is footing the bill, but obviously this isn't accurate. Those perks are being funded by you.

The insurer could cancel the cruise and lower your cost of insurance. Instead, your agent gets to go on a cruise at the expense of your child's 529 college savings plan, or your IRA contributions.

Wouldn't you prefer to purchase your financial products and services from a company that keeps prices low, instead of giving extra perks to sales people who have *already* received hefty commissions for serving you? How many advisors do you think ever say: *You know what, I don't need to go to Bermuda on an all-expense paid trip. Instead, let's refund my clients some of their fees?*

This disturbing observation brings us full circle, with me urging you to do everything possible to minimize your reliance on advisors.

III. Advisor Expertise

Expertise refers to the human capital an advisor has compiled over her career. Some of the credentials that signal expertise include: educational background, licenses, work experience, professional designations, and certifications.

Many advisors have undergraduate degrees. Some also have Masters degrees, including MBAs. Licensing generally does not require a college education. Some professional designations require a university degree, but not all.

The Series 6, 7, 63, and 65 licensing exams are among the most common for financial advisors. These qualification exams are administered by FINRA (the Financial Industry Regulatory Authority). You can find more information on the FINRA website (www.finra.org). These exams are only meant to enforce some *minimal* level of knowledge regarding products, regulations, and risks. Passing an exam does not prove an advisor is capable of providing *good* advice.

There's a broad selection of certifications and designations available to advisors. These are usually bestowed by professional trade organizations on those who complete a series of courses and pass exams. They may require ongoing continuing education credits.

Consider those credentials that appear most relevant for your needs. If you need advice on insurance products, consider a provider with formal credentials in that industry (for example, a Chartered Life Underwriter® or CLU®). If you are seeking accounting advice, consider working with a Certified Public Accountant or CPA. If you are seeking broad assistance across a variety of financial needs, you may want an individual advisor with a Certified Financial Planner or CFP® designation. For in-depth security analysis (examination of individual stocks and bonds), consider a Chartered Financial Analyst or CFA®. There are numerous designations and certifications. Some are more rigorous than others.

While having a particular credential is helpful and a license may be a legal requirement, neither reflects definitive evidence of competence and expertise.

Reclassifying Advisors

There's a lot of information to process when deciding whether to use the services of an advisor, and how to choose one. Given what we've just learned, we can simplify these tasks by re-classifying advisors into five categories, based on what really matters:

1. Skilled, committed, caring advisors who charge fair fees
2. Skilled, committed, caring advisors who charge too much
3. Inept advisors who may be sincerely well-intentioned but just don't know how to do their job properly
4. Conflicted advisors who don't always have clients' best interests at heart
5. Criminals who are out to embezzle and steal client assets

Needless to say, you want to find people in the first category, and avoid all the others. People in the second category may have the requisite skills, but their unjustifiably high fees can do a lot of damage to your nest egg over extended periods. We saw those effects earlier in this book when discussing time value of money and compounding. Over decades, even seemingly small fees (on the order of one percent) can significantly undermine your wealth.

The broader challenge for you is that *all* prospective advisors claim to be in the first category. So how can you distinguish the good, from the bad and the ugly?

Finding Advisors

Good advisors should:

1. Act in your best interest (as fiduciaries)
2. Add value through expert, objective, honest advice
3. Charge reasonable fees commensurate with value added
4. Be there when needed (be accessible and available)

So how do you go about identifying good advisor candidates? You can search on your own or obtain recommendations from people you know and trust. Ideally, recommendations should come from actual clients of the advisor in question, as this means recommenders are personally familiar with the candidate's level of expertise, personal integrity, and fees.

Don't automatically assume an advisor is honest if he's recommended by a friend. The most dangerous con-men are those who insinuate themselves using charm and empty promises throughout an entire network of friends. So, regardless of the source of a recommendation, you should do some research on all candidates. This can be partly accomplished using public records: FINRA's BrokerCheck (finra.org/brokercheck) and the SEC's Investment Adviser Public Disclosure Database (adviserinfo.sec.gov).

An honest advisor will respect your need to do this research, and will openly explain any entries in these records.

Once you identify several decent candidates, you must interview them.

Interviewing Prospective Advisors

Regardless of whether you receive a strong recommendation for an advisor, you should interview multiple candidates representing different firms. The process may take you some time. View it as one of your more important investments.

Below are some interview guidelines. A list of specific questions to ask during interviews may be found at www.PillarsOfWealth.com.

1. Interview at least five advisors. Candidates will likely be thrilled to pitch their services, so it should be easy to set the interviews up at your convenience. Don't let the process drag on too long as that will dilute your learning

2. Confirm that they will act as fiduciaries and ask whether there are circumstances under which they may not be fiduciaries

3. Ask them to explain their fee structure. Do they charge by the hour, by AUM, third party fees, etc.? Keep on the lookout for those compensation mechanisms that can create conflicts of interest

4. Do they receive any rewards or perks for productivity? For example, if they sell certain volumes of insurance or annuities or investment services, could they be eligible to go on vacations paid by insurance companies or other financial services companies?

5. Are they generalists? Assess the *breadth* of their expertise. Can they produce comprehensive financial plans?

6. Are they specialists? Assess the *depth* of their expertise. How much do they know about their professed area of specialization (investing, insurance, college plans, benefits, taxation, estate planning)?

7. What credentials do they have? Do they take any continuing education courses? How do they stay current on changes in products, best practices, and regulations?

8. Which licenses do they have? Are these Federal or State licenses?

9. How much experience do they have in their field? How did they end up working in the industry?

10. Assess whether the advisor is willing to acknowledge (at least philosophically) that advisors themselves are the source of some risk. Arrogant or ignorant advisors will likely deny this

11. Assess the hierarchical structure of the candidate's firm. More hierarchical organizations tend to charge higher fees. For example, brokers working for insurance companies generally have to share investment fees with their organization. In some cases they may be required to give up anywhere from about 30% of their revenue to 70%. If such a broker wanted to earn a (net) 1% fee for herself, she'd have to charge the client somewhere around 1.5%. Needless to say, the client would likely be better off investing through an independent Registered Investment Advisor for significantly lower fees, or going the DIY route at even lower cost

Ask challenging questions (politely) and observe the responses. Does the candidate maintain poise and seem credible? Try to gauge whether the interviewee is trying to motivate you using *greed* or *fear*. Salesmen are taught to leverage these in order to secure business. Be on the lookout for those who use clichés and one-liners. Is the person resorting to these because he lacks depth of knowledge?

Don't Underestimate the Value of These Interviews

The default approach among some busy doctors is to quickly identify one advisor who seems less unpalatable than the others, and to crown that person as winner (or as the lesser of the other evils).

Instead of settling in this way, you can do yourself a great service by recognizing that these sessions are avenues for free learning. But to obtain the desired learning you need multiple exposures. One interview with one advisor is relatively ineffective because it lacks context. Interviews with multiple advisors allow you to identify patterns and hone your critical evaluation skills.

With multiple interviews you can dig deeper. For example, ask the second advisor his opinion about the investment strategy described by the first advisor. Ask the third advisor about the life insurance riders recommended by the second advisor. Instead of making a pitch to you, the advisors now have to critically evaluate each other. This gives you opportunities to see them on the hot seat, and to assess whether they react with integrity.

You can also go back to the first and second advisors and present them with the criticisms you heard in the later interviews. Gauge their reactions. Are their responses credible? Do they get defensive? Do they have the patience to explain their choices to you and address the critiques in detail?

You may initially want to present the opinions to be critiqued as your own rather than having come from other advisors. After you receive some answers reveal that the recommendations came from other professionals. It may be interesting to see whether candidates change their responses once they realize the criticism came from competitors. This can tell you something about their integrity.

If you passively allow advisors to 'pitch you,' you're letting them play their game plan. You can be sure that plan will utilize every subtle method of influence and manipulation known to modern psychology. By driving the interview you remain in control and get a more unrehearsed set of responses.

Review your notes after all the interviews and identify the person who stands out from the crowd. If no one stands out, interview more people.

As already noted, these interviews may well be the most important 'investment' you make. Take them seriously.

Start with a Basic Financial Plan

The interview process will help you identify a leading candidate. If you're looking for a generalist, you can commission the leading candidate to produce a financial plan. The candidate should: act as a fiduciary, have at least a CFP designation, and five to ten years of directly relevant work experience. Ask about these credentials in the initial phone call, and confirm during the interview.

The candidate's plan should give you a clear picture of your financial circumstances and any glaring gaps or deficiencies, such as a need to change investments or add insurance coverage.

Financial plans typically require between 6 to 15 hours of work, which often translates to a total cost of about $2,000 to $4,000. This depends on the complexity of your situation and the hourly rate.

The more information and documents you share, the more comprehensive the results. Working directly with the advisor on the plan gives you an opportunity to assess her professional skills, personal style, and integrity.

Make it clear upfront that the planner is only preparing the financial plan—but not implementing it. This way, she has nothing else at stake and therefore no motivation to 'sell' any particular product. She can focus on creating the best plan for you, as a fiduciary. The resulting plan should ideally encompass all relevant areas, potentially including: retirement, college, and estate planning, as well as insurance, investing, risk management, elder care, etc.

Once the process is complete, you're free to:

1. Take the plan and have it implemented by anyone you choose, including the option of implementing parts of it yourself, or
2. Outsource components of the plan to other specialists. Your generalist may have some good referrals, or
3. In the event the planner offers implementation services, you could even go back to her to implement the plan

The advantage is that having gone through the process, you now have firsthand knowledge of the advisor's capabilities and a personal relationship based on trust and respect.

Of course, you should not mention upfront that you will be allowing her to implement the plan, as that may lead to biased planning recommendations.

The Advisor's Perspective

People are motivated by two things: fear and greed. You need to figure out which one to use on each prospective client.
– Insurance Company Sales Trainer

The most successful advisors are not necessarily those with the best analytical capabilities. They're those with the best influencing skills. And they have numerous opportunities to refine those skills and to embrace the latest psychology and sociology research on effective ways to win clients' trust and influence them to purchase particular products.

To help you understand advisor priorities, consider that a new product presentation from an insurance company or asset management firm to its salesmen often includes segments on:

- These are the client pain points
- These are the things you can say to get the client hooked
- This is how you get paid

Furthermore, advisors generally make a lot more money by gaining *new* clients rather than from servicing existing ones. This is why advisors prefer to spend their time marketing their services to new prospects, rather than spending that time with you. That's one reason why you may find yourself being handed off to the advisor's junior assistant soon after becoming a client. This frees the advisor up to hunt for more client prospects. The junior associate is usually less knowledgeable and less experienced, which can be a problem if you need complex ongoing guidance.

Yes, there are advisors out there who genuinely want to help you, and they're good at their job. But even they will resort to the proven psychological techniques that get you to sign up for their services. Their motivation may be a bit different. It may not be: *I need to manipulate the client so I can make money*. It may instead be: *I'm one of the good guys. I've always bent over backwards for my clients. I'm not manipulating my clients. I'm simply doing what is necessary to ensure they pick me, instead of some crook who will take advantage of them.*

The end result in either case is that you're being manipulated.

Something is Wrong with This Picture

A successful advisor with a large clientele can make a lot more money than a doctor.

Which of them is adding more value to society? The physician/dentist/pharmacist who does pioneering medical research and is paid $150,000 a year, or the advisor who makes $400,000 annually? To me it's just not right that a smooth talker who barely passed a basic licensing exam with a score of 72% is rewarded more than someone who dedicates their entire life's work to science, research, and the wellbeing of others.

I know how much work and dedication is required to be a contributing member of the medical community. I also know how much work and effort is needed to become a financial advisor. There's no comparison.

I'm the first to acknowledge that advisors can add value, but their compensation under our current system is out of sync with the value they actually add. My hope is that financial literacy education will empower doctors to make more decisions on their own. As demand for advisors' services declines, they'll be forced to change their ways: by adding more value and charging less.

Why Advisors Target Medical Professionals?

Here's the answer given by a bewildered bank robber when asked by a judge why he robbed banks: *Because that's where the money is!*

Advisors target medical professionals because doctors are perceived to be wealthier than the average prospect. Financial services providers craft special strategies aimed at physicians and dentists, and their entire approach may focus on taking advantage of a doctor's lack of time to: examine offers carefully or fully understand competitor offerings.

It's generally accepted among the advisory community that doctors make lucrative clients. But they also know it's hard to break into doctors' insular societies, because doctors prefer to seek advice from each other rather than trusting finance professionals. So gaining the trust of doctors is a long process. But advisors have noticed that once they're 'in' with one doctor who trusts and likes them, that same doctor will recommend them to all her friends.

That's the big payoff. And that's why they hound you, mercilessly.

Get a Second Opinion

A patient who feels uncomfortable with medical advice has the choice of seeking a second opinion. Yet many patients feel that getting a second medical opinion somehow betrays or is an insult to the original doctor. But if you're facing a major procedure and don't like any aspect of the initial opinion the right thing to do is to get at least one other opinion.

The same logic applies to financial advice. Even if you've had a long and productive relationship with an advisor, it doesn't hurt to hear other perspectives once in a while. You should certainly get other opinions if you feel uncomfortable with any recommendations you've received.

Your Responsibilities

Medical professionals can't diagnose or treat patients without a physical examination and an opportunity to assess the facts of each case. Similarly, financial advisors need access to you and your records to provide the best advice. A good advisor won't bother you unnecessarily, but will occasionally need your undivided attention to ensure your family's financial well-being is attended to.

So if you choose to work with an advisor, you have some responsibilities. It's up to you to make time to communicate with the advisor and to make available necessary records.

Get your materials together, show up on time to meetings, and turn off your phone so you can give your undivided attention to the advisor. Pay attention, make sure you understand what has been discussed, and make logical decisions. You're not doing this for him. You're doing it for yourself and for your family.

All advisors will try to win your trust. You have a responsibility to identify and reward the good advisors with that trust. The free market theory suggests that if we all do this well, the bad advisors will have no clients and will be forced out of business. That's a good outcome for all consumers.

If You Seek Advice – Find an Expert

As a doctor, you've probably had to convince your patients not to take advice from bloggers or fussy in-laws. Instead, you encourage patients to obtain and follow advice from licensed medical professionals.

The irony, of course, is that doctors often ignore similar advice. Sanford Fisher, CPA, laments that "most physicians don't want to go to professionals. They think they can do it themselves." His partner, Jeffrey Ring, CPA, adds a corollary, "we can tell them [doctors] something over and over and over again but unless and until another physician tells them that same thing they usually won't pay any attention." This corollary reflects a well known fact: doctors value the opinions of their peers. Asking peers for advice seems reasonable for several reasons:

- Doctors are intelligent people
- You trust and respect them
- You can avoid the anxiety and suspicions associated with a financial advisor
- You believe you can save time
- You avoid paying for advice

But despite the best intentions, doctors are generally not trained to be: accountants, attorneys, or financial advisors. The risks of accepting advice from peers include:

- It's unlikely your peer has very broad or very deep knowledge of the matter at hand. She may be a brilliant doctor. But unless she spends every waking moment staying current on all the latest financial planning rules and best practices, she's not a financial expert

- It's unlikely your peer fully understands your circumstances. You may not be comfortable revealing all your personal financial details, and this means the advice you receive may not be appropriate to your specific situation

- Your peer's advice will likely reflect his negative personal experiences and traumas. Just because a product or service didn't work well for him, doesn't automatically mean it's wrong for you and your family

It's very tempting to accept advice from peers. You respect, admire, and trust them. They provide the advice sincerely because they're your friends. But as already noted, accepting their advice opens you up to risks. And so, regardless of how well-intentioned they are, be very careful in accepting such advice.

Ultimately, your most reliable ally is *you*!

The more educated you are, the more you can help yourself, either in making your own decisions, or in finding an expert.

When it's clear you don't have all the answers, get them from reliable professionals. This frees you up to spend more time on your priorities, including family, hobbies, and work. It also decreases the probability that more of your time and money will be wasted later, on fixing problems created by errors you (or your colleague) made in an effort to moonlight as a tax, legal, or financial expert.

Work-Life Balance

The Painful Truth: Physicians Are Not Invincible.

This is the title of an article published in 2000 in the *Southern Medical Journal* by Merry Miller and K. Ramsey McGowen. The article includes a number of telling statistics regarding the difficulties physicians face, including:

> *... physicians are more than twice as likely as the general population to kill themselves ... Female physicians appear to be especially vulnerable. Suicide rates for women physicians are approximately four times that of women in the general population ... The high-risk physician has been described as driven, competitive, compulsive, individualistic, ambitious, and often a graduate of a high-prestige school.*

Many of the serious issues discussed in the article are beyond the scope of this book, but at least one is highly relevant. Citing others, the article states that divorce rates among physicians are as much as twenty percent higher than the general population. Combined with the knowledge that the majority of relationship conflicts are caused by money matters, it's clear that money issues are important to the emotional well-being of doctors and to the success of their relationships.

Take Your Own Advice

Doctors should embrace the advice they give their patients:

- Get some exercise

- Sleep more

- Set boundaries to avoid bringing work home

- Get an annual physical (not one that is self-administered), and

- Connect emotionally with family and friends

Ironically, doctors are very quick to administer this advice to patients, but very slow to adopt it themselves.

Participate in Home Life

No man has ever said on his deathbed, "I wish I'd spent more time at the office."

Over the years, this has been one of my favorite quotes (it's been attributed to many people so I'm unable to cite a specific source).

Occasionally, I insert this saying into conversation. It never fails to be applauded as profound wisdom—except when I'm speaking with certain physicians. On those occasions, the statement is greeted with rebuttals by people I'd describe as driven, competitive, compulsive, individualistic, and ambitious. If this description sounds familiar, you'll find it's the same one in the quote at the beginning of this chapter—the one about those physicians who are at high-risk for self-destructive behavior.

CPA Rajiv Mahajan frequently works with medical practitioners, and his main observation is that too many of them have "zero or very little participation in home life." This inevitably leads to stress, instability, and all too often, divorce. In contrast, those who have a healthy work-life balance spend less time at the office *and most importantly*, Mahajan emphasizes, *are more productive professionally.*

Words of Wisdom

In this section I list various concerns, observations and pearls of wisdom shared over the years by physicians, dentists, and other health care professionals.

Doctors are so used to being taken advantage of and being charged higher prices that they are very defensive and withdraw if they feel they are being cornered by a salesman. Sometimes they withdraw too much.

The greatest barrier to financial learning by doctors is that initially we don't see the subject matter as scientifically rigorous or important ... We don't like to be wrong, and being in a non-medical setting we know little about is humbling— suddenly we don't know as much or more than the people around us. We don't like not knowing as much as others, we don't like admitting it, and it makes us defensive, which comes across to everyone else as arrogance.

Many doctors don't want to ask what the fees are for various financial services because they're uncomfortable, and also because some don't want to know. They fear that the number they hear will be too high, and they don't want to have to deal with the implications of having to find someone new they trust to help them make decisions.

We can be very arrogant or hubristic. We rush into things only to realize we are in over our heads. But it's too late.

We're barely scratching by at the 99th percentile of income. With significant expenditures on private schools for children, large mortgages, insurance, etc., even on decent salaries, it is difficult to make ends meet and save.

We listen too much to our peers—assuming they are experts. But they often don't even know enough to make good decisions for themselves.

Find financial compatibility with your partner/soul mate. Stay as a double earning couple as long as you can.

It feels like our growth has been stunted. We're 37 years old and just beginning to earn decent salaries. Meanwhile our college friends are ten years into successful careers, own their homes, have paid off all their school debt, and saved money for their children's education.

Doctors are notorious Type A personalities, who believe they know best. Many of them mellow over the years as their own fallibility is proven (collapse of family life, financial problems). That hard won wisdom often comes too late.

Doctors' attitude is often: "this advice is better than nothing and we don't have much time to look into it so let's be trusting and hope for the best." Instead, we should proactively make an effort to get good advice. Educate yourself. Don't be intimidated and overwhelmed. Small things you do now will have large impact later.

At the end of medical school, it's really important to learn about budgeting. And it's important to understand compound interest and its effect on student loans or investments.

As doctors we tend to think we can do everything ourselves. So we welcome being given resources and pointed in the right direction for more knowledge. But more often than not (outside the medical setting), this just gives us enough rope to hang ourselves.

Doctors live under a sense of deprivation for so long that they may splurge or over-extend on credit once a bigger salary is available. Need to understand and work toward long term financial goals.

Many doctors have lots of life insurance, but few have enough disability insurance. We're more likely to become disabled than to die prematurely. Get DI to protect your income stream.

When you need it, "disability insurance is worth its weight in gold."

Doctors share a trait: Drivenness, which often means "I can do anything." Sometimes that can hurt them if they don't fully understand how financial markets and institutions work. Doctors need to fight some of those impulses. Otherwise they can make bad investments and/or end up being highly leveraged [owing too much money].

The problem with doctors is that they can be too busy, too stubborn, or too proud.

Doctors don't get told 'no' a lot. So we engage in conspicuous consumption instead of paying off debts or investing in their practice.

Some doctors react with arrogance to advice: "I'm a doctor and you're not, so I'm going to do it my way." This may be okay in a medical setting, but outside it, this can be very costly for us.

We're sitting ducks! We know we need to make certain financial decisions, and we feel the clock is ticking. Lots of salesmen target us, but we don't know where to start.

Try to know what you don't know.

Strive for life balance.

Don't try to keep up with the Joneses: it's a never-ending and futile effort. You'll always feel you're competing and playing catch up. It's human nature to compete on social standing, but resist it. It won't make you happy.

Live below your means. Save. Prepare. Be modest.

Building Pillars Requires Advance Planning

Any architect, engineer, or construction worker knows that plans are crucial. No one wants to have to tear down a wall (or pillar) and start again, especially when proper planning (blueprints, disciplined construction) can obviate the need for such backtracking.

In the introduction to this book I stated three axioms:

1. Your most valuable asset is earning capacity
2. Your most precious resource is time
3. Your greatest enemy is procrastination

Thoughtful planning automatically embraces each of these tenets: It respects and protects your earning capacity, recognizes time constraints, and avoids procrastination.

Aside: Plans are even more crucial for owners of private medical practices, because unlike other business owners in other industries, where the spouse can take over the business, only properly licensed doctors/dentists can own medical/dental practices. So the option of having a family member step in and run the practice is often not available. In such circumstances, there must be some contingency planning in place.

Benefits of Advanced Planning

Consider the case of a surgeon with three young daughters. He faces the future cost of three college educations and three weddings.

Where's that money going to come from? What if in addition to college costs, the children must be sent to private schools because local public schools are not very good? He doesn't want his children to be paralyzed by debt when they graduate from college, but he doesn't know how to arrange things such that tuition isn't sucking the family's savings away. He doesn't know how much insurance is enough or too much. He doesn't know how to invest systematically.

This scenario is based on a true story, and many households face similar challenges. Some people respond by putting decisions off, and only re-engaging when the challenges can no longer be ignored—often when it's too late to make good decisions.

Instead of reacting to circumstances, it's better to plan proactively. A doctor earning the average surgeon's salary should be able to meet all these financial challenges successfully. But only if he follows a disciplined plan beginning early in his career.

Proper planning sets you up for success by ensuring that:

1. Your debts are covered (through full understanding of debt repayment options and the dangers of becoming over-extended)
2. You have plans in place in the event of disability or premature death
3. You have a plan in place to fund children's education expenses (and weddings)
4. You have a solid sense of the financial products and estate planning tools needed to meet your family's needs
5. You know your assets are as safe as you can make them
6. Your taxes are minimized
7. Your savings are maximized (and you avoid questionable investments)
8. You know your assets will reach intended heirs or other destinations (in a tax-efficient manner)
9. You're able to retire sooner rather than later
10. You feel financially secure and you don't lose sleep over money issues

In medical terms, the point of advance planning, and of this entire book, is that *preventative medicine is far more effective than reactive medicine.* It's far easier to anticipate financial needs and dangers than it is to clean up the mess after disasters strike.

Do your family a favor—plan ahead!

Many doctors can't plan ahead because they don't know where to start. This book provides that starting point with a basic education on the major financial planning issues. My hope is that by defining the universe of necessary knowledge, and helping you get your arms around it, you'll gain enough confidence to get started. Once you begin with some financial decisions, the rest will become progressively easier.

I hope this book will help you build some much needed momentum in your decision making, and I wish you and your family happiness and prosperity.

Appendix 1: Personal (Household) Budgets

A budget is a tool for tracking income and expenditures over some specified period of time, for example, over a month or a year. Tracking how much money you receive (income) versus how much you pay (expenditures), allows you to estimate whether you have any money left over (for saving or investing) or whether you need to borrow to make ends meet (use credit cards, get a bank loan, or borrow from family). If you're constantly borrowing—you're over-extended! You've got to make some changes to ensure you are living within your means. Usually, this means cutting down on expenses.

In this appendix, a customized budget is provided for each major stage of your development. Some assumptions are made at each stage. For example, I assume marriage and birth of children take place during the Internship/Residency/Fellowship phase. Your circumstances may, of course, differ.

For your convenience, spreadsheet versions of these are available on the website at www.PillarsOfWealth.com.

Budget Instructions

The first step is to maintain good records. Your pay stub(s) will list your income and sometimes a few deductibles or expenses. Receipts, bank, and credit card statements will help you identify other expenses. You should develop a habit of saving all transaction records. When asked by a vendor if you need a receipt—always say yes. Then put all the receipts in one place. You or your accountant can sort through them later. If the IRS decides to challenge your accounting choices, it's crucial to have receipts backing up your tax filings.

A Budget usually tells you how much you earned and spent over the *last* year (or month). If you want a *future* budget forecast, you can use projected or estimated earnings and expense numbers.

Medical Student Budget

Budget Item	Dollar Amount
INCOME SOURCES "Income" from student loans * Gifts/loans from family Part time job Other **TOTAL INCOME**	
EXPENDITURES Rent/mortgage payments Utilities (gas, electric, water, sewer, trash) Internet/cable/satellite All phones Food Clothing Personal care/medical expenses Car maintenance (repairs/oil changes) Commuting costs (parking/fuel/tolls) Insurance (health/dental/auto/renter's/life/disability) Travel, dining out, entertainment Moving expenses to residency destination Other **TOTAL EXPENDITURES**	
NET INCOME = **Total Income** minus **Total Expenditures**	

* Student loans are not truly income, but they are a source of funds.

You can create a monthly budget, but an annual time frame makes the most sense as it ensures you capture expenses that occur only once or twice a year. Make sure all the figures are annual equivalents. For example, if you have a monthly car payment, multiply it by 12 for the annual budget.

Enter gross salary under Income, and the various tax, Social Security and other deductions under the appropriate headings. Make sure you include income from all sources. (This information should be shown on your pay stubs).

Then input and sum up all expenditures. The difference between Total Income and Total Expenditures is known as Net Income. If Net Income is negative, then instead of saving, you are over-extended and must borrow or tap your existing savings to cover your costs.

It can be useful to identify those expenses that are *discretionary* (i.e., optional). These are the first ones you should cut back if you find yourself over-extended. Typical candidates are expenses in the travel, dining out, and entertainment categories.

Intern/Resident/Fellow Budget

Budget Item	Dollar Amount
INCOME SOURCES	
Salary	
Moonlighting/other income	
Gifts/loans from family	
Part time job	
Other	
TOTAL INCOME	
DEDUCTIONS FROM INCOME	
All Taxes	
Social Security	
401(k) or 403(b) contributions	
TOTAL DEDUCTIONS FROM INCOME	
INCOME AFTER DEDUCTIONS	
= Total Income minus Deductions	
EXPENDITURES	
Rent/mortgage payments	
Student debt payments	
Utilities (gas, electric, water, sewer, trash)	
Internet/cable/satellite	
All phones	
Food	
Clothing	
Day care costs/Private school tuition	
Personal care/medical expenses	
Car maintenance (repairs/oil changes)	
Commuting costs (parking/fuel/tolls)	
Insurance (health/dental/auto/renter's/life/disability)	
Travel, dining out, entertainment	
Moving expenses to first job destination	
Wedding expenses	
Contract attorney and accountant fees	
Other	
TOTAL EXPENDITURES	
NET INCOME	

First 'Real' Job Budget

Budget Item	Dollar Amount
INCOME	
Salary	
Moonlighting/other income	
Child Support/alimony received	
Gifts/loans from family	
Dividends, interest, capital gains	
Rental property income	
Other	
TOTAL INCOME	
DEDUCTIONS FROM INCOME	
All Taxes *	
Social Security	
401(k) or 403(b) contributions	
Other	
TOTAL DEDUCTIONS FROM INCOME	
INCOME AFTER DEDUCTIONS	
= Total Income minus Deductions	
EXPENDITURES	
Rent/mortgage payments	
Student debt payments	
Child support/alimony paid	
Association or condo fees	
Utilities (gas, electric, water, sewer, trash)	
Internet/cable/satellite	
All phones	
Food	
Clothing	
Day care costs	
Private school tuition	
Personal care/medical expenses	
Car maintenance (repairs/oil changes)	
Commuting costs (parking/fuel/tolls)	
continued on next page …	

continued from previous page ...

Insurance (health/dental/auto/renter's/life/disability)
Charitable contributions
Travel, dining out, entertainment
Moving expenses to first job destination
Estate planning attorney and accountant fees
Costs of starting up a new practice
Contract attorney and accountant fees
Other
TOTAL EXPENDITURES

NET INCOME
= Income After Deductions minus Expenditures

* Your pay stub should indicate the various taxes that have been deducted from your income. These should be included in the Deductions from Income section, above. This total is usually a reflection of choices you made on your W-4 form, in which you estimated the number of allowances for which you expected to be eligible during the year. At year's end you file your tax forms, and those calculations reveal whether you still owe more tax or are eligible for a tax refund. Your true Net Income for the year should reflect any additional taxes or refunds. Once you have an estimate of this adjustment, include it in the All Taxes entry.

An alternative to the representation above is to remove All Taxes from the Deductions from Income section, and instead include them under Expenditures, where once again you estimate the full tax bill for the entire year (paystub deductions adjusted for taxes payable or refundable).

Manager/Owner Budget

Note: this budget is for your <u>personal household</u> finances. It is not meant to capture budget items for your private practice. Business financial statements are covered in *Finance and Business Essentials for Medical Practices*, the second book of the *Pillars of Wealth* series.

Budget Item	Dollar Amount
INCOME	
Salary plus Bonus	
Profit sharing revenue	
Moonlighting/other income	
Child Support/alimony received	
Gifts/loans from family	
Dividends, interest, capital gains	
Rental property income	
Other	
TOTAL INCOME	
DEDUCTIONS FROM INCOME	
All Taxes	
Social Security	
401(k) or 403(b) contributions	
Other	
TOTAL DEDUCTIONS FROM INCOME	
INCOME AFTER DEDUCTIONS	
= Total Income minus Deductions	
EXPENDITURES	
Rent/mortgage payments	
Student debt payments	
Child support/alimony paid	
Association or condo fees	
Utilities (gas, electric, water, sewer, trash)	
Internet/cable/satellite	
<div align="center">continued on next page ...</div>	

continued from previous page ...

All phones
Food
Clothing
Day care costs
Private school tuition
Personal care/medical expenses
Car maintenance (repairs/oil changes)
Commuting costs (parking/fuel/tolls)
Insurance (health/dental/auto/renter's/life/disability)
Charitable contributions
Travel, dining out, entertainment
Business education seminars
Moving expenses to new job destination
Estate planning attorney and accountant fees
Costs of starting up a new practice
Contract attorney and accountant fees
Other

TOTAL EXPENDITURES

NET INCOME
= Income After Deductions minus Expenditures

Appendix 2: Basic Economics Concepts

This section serves as an economics primer. Many basic and some more advanced concepts are defined in a sequence that might be used in an introductory class.

Economics

According to the American Economic Association, economics is "the study of scarcity, the study of how people use resources, or the study of decision-making." Wikipedia provides this definition, "Economics is the social science that analyzes the production, distribution, and consumption of goods and services." A *good* or 'product' is a tangible commodity or output you can touch and feel. Goods may be produced, purchased, sold or traded. They may be intended for final use by a consumer (for example, a lawn mower, chocolate chip cookie, tongue depressor, Magnetic Resonance Imaging machine), or they may be used as inputs into creation of other goods. A *service* is any work or task that is performed for someone. Unlike goods, services are intangible in that they cannot be touched or felt. Examples are consulting services provided by an attorney, accountant, dentist or physician.

Consumers

The people who use goods and services.

Scarcity

Because all things in life are scarce (that is, their supply is limited), we're constantly forced to make choices, trading off some things for others.

Wants

Those products and services we *desire* to have. See Needs, below.

Needs

The basic requirements for survival, which include shelter, food and water. Many people confuse *wants* with *needs*. If you wish to live within or below your means, your decisions should be based more on need and less on want.

Factors of Production and Resources

Factors of production are the assets or inputs required to produce goods and services. They include:

1. Land, including natural resources such as iron, tin, magnesium, timber, etc.
2. Capital, which is the fancy word economists use for money (that is, dollars invested)
3. Labor, which refers to man-hours contributed by humans

The typical mechanism is that investors put up capital (money), which is used to lease land, buy the various inputs needed for production, build a factory, buy equipment, pay for labor (people's wages), and produce goods (products). Sales of these goods provide revenue which is, in turn, used to pay for more labor and to cover other expenses (purchase of all other inputs) required to make more goods (products). When a company is self-sustaining, it's generating enough revenue to cover all expenditures, and any money left over is profit available to be paid to the firm's owners, sometimes in the form of dividends.

We often consider the total availability of these factors of production to a single nation. These assets or inputs are used by that nation to produce what is needed (or wanted) by its citizens. Because these factors of production are scarce (they're not available in infinite quantities) each nation has to make decisions about how it will prioritize the use of its factors or assets. The decisions faced by each nation are:

1. Which goods and services to produce?
2. How to produce these goods and services?
3. Whom these goods and services should be produced for?

Note that a single corporation or local government such as a city or county must also make comparable choices given the resources it has available and the services it's considering making available to its residents.

In *free market* economies, the answers to these questions are provided by the free interaction of investors and consumers. That is, the demand by price conscious consumers for goods and services, combined by supply constraints and the profit motive of investors and entrepreneurs determines which products and services will be available, to whom they will be available, and at what prices.

In contrast, centrally-controlled economies (known as *command economies*) dictate supply and prices in prescribed ways instead of allowing market forces to determine prices (examples are the Communist regime of the former Soviet Union and the current authoritarian regime in North Korea).

From a macro-economic (big picture) American healthcare perspective, we know there are limited resources. Therefore, tradeoffs must be accepted in the practice of medicine, just as they are accepted elsewhere. As our federal and state governments have gone deeper into debt, this has meant (and will likely continue to mean) that there will be less money available in future (per capita) to provide medical services. In turn, the implication is that doctors will have to get comfortable with change, and potentially reduced financial compensation. It's also why making better decisions is more crucial than ever, because there's less margin for error in providing for your family and funding your retirement. Under these constrained circumstances procrastination and poor decisions will be more harmful and their negative effects harder than ever to reverse.

Conspicuous Consumption

The use of a good or service with the intent of impressing others.

Value

An assignment of worth which is typically based on the utility (usefulness) or scarcity of the item in question.

Utility

Utility is the capacity to be useful. Economists have an obscure unit of measure for utility, known as *utils*, although it's rarely possible to quantify utility other than making relative statements.

The Paradox of Value

This refers to our tendency to assign the lowest value to our most crucial needs for survival such as water and air, and the highest value to those things we need the least, such as gold and diamonds.

Wealth

The modern definition is the abundance of assets, resources and material possessions. That is, our wealth is the sum of the tangible items we own. More philosophical interpretations suggest that our wealth goes beyond material goods.

Efficiency

A relative term referring to how optimally resources are used to produce goods or services. An efficient individual, company, or nation is characterized by fewer wasted resources than a less efficient individual, company, or nation.

Supply and Demand

Demand refers to the quantities of a good or service that consumers are willing to buy at various market prices. *Supply* refers to the quantities of a good or service that suppliers are willing to provide at various market prices. In a competitive marketplace, the interplay between demand and supply determines market prices. When demand for a product is much greater than its supply the product's price is likely to be high. When supply is greater than demand, we expect the product's price to be low.

Productivity

The rate at which goods or services are produced by an individual, company, nation, etc. Often measured as the output produced divided by the inputs required, where the latter include labor and capital.

The American capitalist economy is believed to be relatively productive compared to other nations because:

1. We use our resources relatively efficiently
2. We specialize to increase efficiency and productivity
3. We invest in Human Capital (our labor pool)

Price Elasticity of Demand and Supply

These are measures of how responsive consumers and suppliers of goods and services are to price changes. A product with high price elasticity is one whose demand or supply moves significantly when there is a price change. In such cases even a small price reduction could lead to much greater demand or much lower supply. Conversely, a product with low elasticity of demand and supply will exhibit small changes in demand or supply as prices change.

Monopoly

A monopoly exists when a single company controls effectively all of the market for a product or service. Monopolies are thus characterized by a lack of economic competition. This is what a pharmaceutical company becomes whenever it obtains patent protection over a drug. The patent prevents the introduction of competing drugs, depriving consumers of competitive market forces that can ordinarily be relied upon to reduce prices. Thus, a monopolist can raise prices significantly, and since consumers have nowhere else to turn (especially for a very important medication), they are forced to pay the high price. Under these circumstances, the drug in question has low price elasticity. Despite significant increases in price, demand does not decline much.

Substitutes & Complements

It's easiest to define these terms using examples. Consider the following scenario which begins with the wages of hospital physicians going up. In response, hospital administrators hire more nurse practitioners and transfer some physicians' duties to the nurse practitioners. The subsequent higher demand for nurse practitioners causes their average wages to increase. In this example, physicians and nurse practitioners are known as *substitutes*. That is, when the price of the former goes up, demand for, and price of, the latter go up. Hospital administrators *substitute* nurse practitioners for physicians.

Now a different mechanism: the prices of smart phones decline. In response, more consumers buy smart phones *and* accessories, which means higher demand and prices for earphones. In this scenario, smart phones and earphones are complements. That is, more purchases of the former are *complemented* (or accompanied) by more purchases of the latter.

Diminishing Marginal Utility

Consider Patient X, who was just admitted to the emergency room, having almost bled out due to a stab wound. Patient X's survival depends to a great extent on quick replenishment of blood. Following arrival at the hospital, he receives treatment including a blood transfusion amounting to five units of blood. Which of those five units provided the most benefit to him? The first or the last? The first unit of blood is the one that pulls him back from the brink of death, the second also has a significant net (or marginal) effect, but slightly less than the first one. The third unit provides additional benefit, but less than the second unit, and so on. The last unit might help a bit, but at that point the additional benefit is relatively small, and no longer a matter of life and death.

This is an example of diminishing marginal utility (of blood). The first unit of a good or a service has a big effect. That is, it gives us great utility or usefulness. The second unit is still quite useful, but on the margin, that addition's utility or benefit is smaller than the first unit's. Each subsequent unit provides a smaller amount of utility. In other words, the utility diminishes as we receive more and more of a good.

Economists are interested in concepts such as: diminishing marginal utility of consumption (the tenth donut you eat is less satisfying than the first) and the diminishing marginal utility of wealth (the tenth million saved is less satisfying than the first million dollars saved).

Variable Cost

These are costs that vary with the level of production. For example, the amount of raw material utilized and hours of employed labor increase as production is increased in a factory. In a medical context, the more surgeries a surgeon performs, the more gauze pads, sutures, and other products are used up.

Fixed Cost

These are the costs that don't vary with the level of production, for example, rent and property taxes.

Average Cost

The average cost for a particular good or service is obtained by dividing the total cost for all the units produced by the number of units produced.

Marginal Cost

The marginal cost is the cost of the last unit produced. In many cases, the more units are produced, the less each subsequent one costs, which leads to a situation of diminishing marginal cost.

Marginal Benefit

The marginal benefit is the benefit or utility derived from the last unit received, purchased, or consumed.

Competition

A rivalry in which every buyer and seller seeks to get the most advantageous price for goods and services sought or offered.

Comparative Advantage

Some individuals, companies or nations have particular advantages in terms of factors of production (labor, land, capital) which gives them an efficiency advantage in making certain goods or offering certain services. For example, in recent decades Southeast Asia has benefited from its comparative advantage of cheap labor.

Rational Expectations

Traditional economic theory assumes that market participants including consumers, producers, and middlemen of various sorts all make decisions logically. This is an appealing assumption until one takes a closer look at the strict definition of *rationality*.

Under the strict economic definition, rationality means that for the purpose of decision making, we're all identical to Star Trek's Mr. Spock: we always consider all relevant information, we always come to the logical conclusion regarding that information, and we never ever act emotionally.

One criticism of this rationality assumption is that if it's true, economic bubbles shouldn't happen. This is because we should all be able to logically observe that asset prices have appreciated unreasonably, and our subsequent actions would then bring prices back into alignment well before a bubble has the chance to form—let alone burst.

Nevertheless, the assumption that market participants have rational expectations regarding the economy and asset prices remains a fixture of classical economic thought.

Behavioral Economics

Behavioral economics is a (relatively recent) field of study which allows for emotional or non-rational behavior on the part of market participants. This field is heavily influenced by the psychology literature which has documented many psychological biases in which humans clearly don't think or act logically. Unlike the traditional assumption of rationality, behavioral economics easily explains asset bubbles and other human decision making inconsistencies.

Incentives

Incentives are expected rewards (or punishments) that motivate people to certain actions. Consumers, employees, patients, colleagues, and suppliers all respond to incentives. If the incentives are compelling, we have the relevant population's undivided attention. The less compelling the incentives, the less likely the population is to act in the desired fashion.

Time Value of Money

This key concept is discussed under Axiom 3 earlier in this book. It's based on the idea that a dollar received today can be invested to yield a *Future Value* which is greater than a dollar. Suppose you receive $1 today. You can invest that dollar at an interest rate 'r' and the future value of that $1 can be calculated as follows

$$\text{Future Value} = \$1(1+r)$$

Discounting

I recommend reviewing the Time Value of Money section provided earlier in the book prior to reading about discounting.

We know that under ordinary circumstances, a dollar received today will be worth more than a dollar received in the future. This is because we can invest today's dollar at some interest rate, say 5%, and receive $1(1+.05) = $1.05 at year's end.

What is a future dollar worth today? The logic described above tells us that today's value must be less than one dollar (and will grow to a full dollar over the course of a year due to interest received over the year). That value may be calculated as follows

$$\text{(Dollar amount invested today)}(1+.05) = \$1 \text{ in future}$$

This can be easily manipulated to yield

$$\text{Dollar amount invested today} = \frac{\$1}{(1+.05)}$$

The right side of this equation represents the discounted value of that one dollar, or its *Present Value* (PV). In this case it's discounted at a rate of 5% over one year.

If the rate of interest is 8%, the equation becomes

$$PV = \frac{\$1}{(1+.08)}$$

If the investment is over 2 years (instead of one year) at 8% annually, the equation is

$$PV = \frac{\$1}{(1+.08)^2}$$

Generally for a cash flow received 'T' years in the future with prevailing interest rate or *Discount Rate,* 'r'

$$Present\ Value = \frac{cash\ flow\ generated\ in\ year\ T}{(1+r)^T}$$

In summary, any dollar amount to be received (or paid) in the future can be discounted to provide an equivalent value in today's dollars. That discounted value is referred to as the Present Value of the future cash flow. If you are examining a stream of cash flows in future, for example, expected earnings by your medical practice over the next five years, you can discount each of the cash flows and then sum those up to obtain a Present Value of all those cash flows combined. This technique is often used in valuing businesses, including medical practices.

As a general rule, the rate used in discounting, 'r,' must account for the riskiness of the promised future cash flow. So discounting a very safe cash flow such as interest promised by a very safe company would require a low value of 'r.' In contrast, a very risky cash flow such as that promised by a small and unstable company would require the use of a higher value of 'r'. The Present Value becomes smaller the larger the value of 'r.'

A Financial Security

A financial security is an instrument (for example: a stock or bond) that represents some financial value. Securities may be issued by corporations or government organizations. The most familiar securities are stocks issued by publicly listed corporations, which may be bought or sold through a stock exchange such as the New York Stock Exchange.

Valuation

Valuation refers to the process of calculating financial value. Valuation usually involves calculation of the Present Value of all cash flows associated with an asset. That asset can be a power plant, a factory, a medical practice, a stock or bond issued by a corporation, etc. The time value of money concept is used to apply discounting to future cash flows, converting them to present value equivalents. The discount rate takes into account all sources of risk

$$\text{Present Value} = \frac{cash\ flow\ generated\ in\ year\ t}{(1+r)^t}$$

Where r = risk free rate plus a risk premium accounting for the riskiness of the cash flow.

To this point all our calculations have assumed individual (single) future cash flows. Multiple cash flows can be converted to an all-encompassing present value using

$$\text{Present Value} = \sum_{t=1}^{T} \frac{cash\ flow\ generated\ in\ year\ t}{(1+r)^t}$$

In this equation we account for a total of 'T' cash flows, each discounted by the rate 'r' over the appropriate span of time.

Net Present Value (NPV)

How do you decide whether to embark on a project (for example, purchase an existing practice)? You would estimate the net earnings (future cash flows) the new practice would produce. Since there's uncertainty involved, you can't expect to know exactly what these values would be. To account for this uncertainty, discount the cash flows by an interest rate 'r' that contains an appropriate risk premium. Next, subtract the value of the initial investment, as follows

$$\text{NPV} = \sum_{t=1}^{T} \frac{cash\ flow\ generated\ in\ year\ t}{(1+r)^t} - \text{INV}_0$$

Where INV_0 is the initial investment (at time 0, which by definition is the present, i.e., now).

If there are multiple outflows, for example, if we need to invest additional funds over several years, we include those outflows as additional terms (preceded by negative signs) in the NPV calculation (appropriately discounted)

$$NPV = \sum_{t=1}^{T} \frac{cash\ flow\ generated\ in\ year\ t}{(1+r)^t} - INV_0 - \frac{INV_1}{(1+r)^1} - \frac{INV_2}{(1+r)^2}$$

The NPV Decision Rule

Accept all projects or investments whose NPV > 0.
Reject all projects or investments whose NPV < 0.

Interest

The interest rate reflects the cost of borrowing or the return on lending. When you borrow to finance your education or medical practice, you must pay the lender (bank or government) for the use of its money. When you lend to others, you will demand a return on your investment in the form of interest payments.

A typical consumer pays a higher rate for borrowing than she could get for lending. Think about what the bank pays you in interest on your checking account (close to zero!) and compare that to what the bank charges you to finance your home or car purchases or to carry a balance on your credit card (anywhere from about 5% to 25% or more!).

Inflation

Inflation is the general increase in prices, or alternatively, the decrease in the purchasing power of your money. While inflation can be negative (*deflation*), in most economies positive inflation is the norm. Inflation is the reason why it's generally inadvisable to hide money under the proverbial mattress. This is because that money steadily loses its value or purchasing power. To keep up with inflation, it's better to put your money into some interest-earning assets (a savings account, certificate of deposit, or a more aggressive investment with higher return and risk characteristics). We should all seek a rate of return which is at least as high as inflation, in order to avoid having our money lose its purchasing power.

Purchasing Power

A good way to understand purchasing power is to think of it as the amount of goods or services that can be purchased with a single dollar. That single dollar will buy fewer and fewer goods and services as inflation causes the prices of those items to increase over time. You want your investments to grow at a rate that is faster than inflation so you can realize some real gains with respect to the cost of living.

Nominal interest rate

The interest rates we see advertised by financial institutions or car dealers are typically stated in nominal terms. These are the actual rates we pay (receive) to borrow (lend). This contrasts with Real interest rates which are explained below.

Real interest rate

The Real interest rate is approximately the difference between the stated nominal rate and the inflation rate. A simplistic representation of this relationship is as follows

Real interest rate = Nominal interest rate − Inflation rate

Thus, the Real rate is, as the name implies, the true return on investment or cost of borrowing once we've adjusted for inflation. If the nominal rate of return on an investment is 7% and the inflation over that period is 4%, then the real return is 7 − 4 = 3%. This 3% is the actual change in our purchasing power.

Investing

The term *investing* is often understood to mean purchasing of individual stocks and bonds or mutual and exchange traded funds in retirement plans (IRAs and 401(k)). But 'investing' is much broader. It includes direct investments in unlisted corporations, acting as an angel investor in very early stage companies, participating in private equity or hedge fund ventures, etc. In fact, it applies to any situation in which you are spending money with a view to receiving some positive return in future.

Tax

A tax is a financial burden or levy imposed on a wage-earner, property owner, corporation, etc., in order to support a government (local, state, or federal).

The Dismal Science

The field of economics has often been called the dismal science. This has historically been the case for two reasons: (1) economics often appears to be less scientifically rigorous than fields such as physics and biology because precise statements are difficult to make. (2) When you see two economists interviewed on television, they often argue diametrically opposed positions to the point of apoplexy, and there's no way to determine who is right or wrong.

In fairness, however, significant advances have been made over the past half-century. Yes, economists can be seen arguing opposite predictions until they're blue in the face, and economic predictions are often wrong, *and* you can almost set your clock by the booms and busts and financial shenanigans reported in the media. But we do know a lot more about asset pricing, human behavior, and economic decision making than ever before. In recent decades the dismal science has become more disciplined and more quantitative.

Keep in mind that not so long ago anyone practicing medicine was in danger of being branded a witch, or that for centuries medicine's primary method of treating patients involved the use of leeches. My point is that doctors—people of hard science—often dismiss economic and business principles on the grounds that they are non-scientific and therefore worthless. But all sciences require centuries to grow and mature.

It's true that social sciences lack perfectly controlled experiments with precisions measured to nanometers or micro liters. But statistical principles do allow practitioners of these sciences to discover and make progress, just as they do in any other science. Somewhat similarly, medicine also doesn't have all the answers. Despite huge advances, we still don't understand many biological processes. This obviously doesn't make medicine irrelevant—it merely reminds us that science is a process of ongoing discovery. Two steps forward, one step back.

In any case, the point of this commentary is not to convince you to become an economist. Rather, it's a reminder that the fields of economics and finance can tell us some important things we need to know. And they can also help us to identify what we don't know.

It's not Rocket Science

While the study of economics does require intellect, economics is generally not rocket science. If you survived organic chemistry, you have the intellectual capacity to understand economic principles.

Most traditional economics concepts can be handled with high school mathematics. The upshot is that if you are sufficiently motivated and have the time, you can learn as much as you want about economics and finance.

References and Online Resources

References

"Malpractice Insurance." American College of Physicians.
http://www.acponline.org/residents_fellows/career_counseling/
malpractice_insurance.htm

Arnow, F. Michael and George C. Xakellis, Jr. "Making Your Balance
Sheet Work for You." *Family Practice Management,* 6 (2001): 27-31.
http://www.aafp.org/fpm/2001/0600/p27.html#fpm20010600
p27-ut1

Bar-Or, Yuval. "Empowering Physicians with Financial Literacy,"
Journal of Medical Practice Management, July/August, 2015.

Bar-Or, Yuval. "Understanding Uncertainty and Common Risk
Management Challenges," *Investments & Wealth Monitor,*
March/April 2015.

Brafman, Ori, and Rom Brafman. *Sway: the Irresistible Pull of Irrational
Behavior.* New York: Doubleday, 2008.

Carmon, Ziv and Dan Ariely. "Focusing on the Foregone: How Value Can Appear So Different to Buyers and Sellers." *Journal of Consumer Research*, 27 (2000): 360-370.

Choate, Natalie. *Life & Death Planning for Retirement Benefits*. Ataxplan Publications, 2011.

Cutler, David, Elizabeth Wikler, and Peter Basch. "Reducing Administrative Costs and Improving the Health Care System." *New England Journal of Medicine*, 2012; 367:1875-1878.

Fresne, Julie A. and James Youngclaus. "Physician Education Debt and the Cost to Attend Medical School, 2012 Update." *Association of American Medical Colleges*, February 2013. https://www.aamc.org/download/328322/data/statedebtreport.pdf

Gladwell, Malcolm. "Cocksure: Banks, Battles, and the Psychology of Overconfidence." *The New Yorker*, 27 July 2009.

Jena, Anupam B., Seth Seabury, Darius Lakdawalla, and Amitabh Chandra. "Malpractice Risk According to Physician Specialty." *New England Journal of Medicine*, 365.7 (2011): 629-636.

Miller, Merry N., Ramsey McGowen, and James Quillen. "The Painful Truth: Physicians Are Not Invincible." *Southern Medical Journal*, 93.10 (2000).

"Dealing with Medical Education Debt." The New England Journal of Medicine Career Center. http://www.nejmcareercenter.org/article/dealing-with-medical-education-debt/

Riepenhoff, Jill, and Mike Wagner. "Fear of Loan Debt Grows for Dentists, Doctors." *The Columbus Dispatch*, 17 December 2012. http://www.dispatch.com/content/stories/local/2012/12/17/fear-of-loan-debt-grows-for-dentists-doctors.html

Youngclaus, James A., Paul A. Koehler, Laurence J. Kotlikoff, and John M. Wiecha, "Can Medical Students Afford to Choose Primary Care? An Economic Analysis of Physician Education Debt Repayment." *Academic Medicine*, 88.1 (2013): 16-25. 16 Nov. 2012.
http://journals.lww.com/academicmedicine/Fulltext/2013/0100 0/Can_Medical_Students_Afford_to_Choose_Primary.15.aspx

Zweig, Jason. *Your Money & Your Brain: How the New Science of Neuroeconomics Can Help Make You Rich*. New York: Simon & Schuster, 2007.

Online Resources

The American Dental Association collects revenue, expense, and net income data for dental practices.
http://www.ada.org/en/science-research/health-policy-institute/data-center/dental-practice

The American Medical Association's mission is "to promote the art and science of medicine and the betterment of public health."
http://www.ama-assn.org

The Association of American Medical Colleges FIRST program is "designed to help members of the academic medicine community navigate the complexities of financial aid, student debt, and money management." https://www.aamc.org/services/first/

BankRate.com – Rent vs. Buy real estate calculator.
http://www.bankrate.com/calculators/mortgages/rent-or-buy-home.aspx

The College Savings Plans Network serves as a clearinghouse for information among state-administered college savings programs.
http://www.collegesavings.org

Federal Student Aid, an office of the U.S. Department of Education, provides information on loans and repayments. https://studentaid.ed.gov/sa/

Federal Trade Commission – on choosing a credit counselor. https://www.consumer.ftc.gov/articles/0153-choosing-credit-counselor

FICO tips for improving your credit score: http://www.myfico.com/crediteducation/improveyourscore.aspx

Financial Industry Regulatory Authority (FINRA) is an independent, not-for-profit organization authorized by Congress to protect America's investors. Among other duties, it administers various licensing or qualification exams for financial market professionals. http://www.finra.org/industry/qualification-exams.

FINRA's BrokerCheck tool tracks current licensing status and history, employment history and any reported regulatory, customer dispute, criminal and other matters for all registered brokers. It also takes disciplinary action against brokers who break the rules. http://brokercheck.finra.org

IBRinfo was created by the nonprofit, nonpartisan Project on Student Debt to help student borrowers. http://www.ibrinfo.org

The Medical Group Management Association (MGMA) aims to equip medical practice leaders with information and tools needed for success. The organization also collects and compiles compensation data for medical practices. http://www.mgma.com/industry-data/overview

Medscape provides medical news, professional education, CMEs and compensation data for physicians. http://www.medscape.com/sites/public/physician-comp/2016

The National Student Loan Data System (NSLDS) is the U.S. Department of Education's central database for student aid. http://www.nslds.ed.gov/nslds_SA/

The *Pillars of Wealth* initiative aims to equip medical professionals with a high quality, unbiased education they can use to make better financial and business decisions for themselves, their families, and their medical practices. http://pillarsofwealth.com/

The Small Business Administration (SBA) counsels, assists and protects the interests of small businesses. It provides a broad array of material for existing and prospective small business owners, including advice on choosing a business structure. https://www.sba.gov/starting-business/choose-your-business-structure

The Social Security Administration provides a broad array of services, including a Retirement Estimator. https://www.ssa.gov/retire/estimator.html

U.S. Department of Energy provides, among its many services, a source for fuel economy information. http://www.fueleconomy.gov/feg/drive.shtml

Zillow.com provides listings and real estate closing cost estimates. http://www.zillow.com/mortgage-learning/closing-costs/

Books by Yuval Bar-Or

Pillars of Wealth I: Personal Finance Essentials for Medical Professionals

Pillars of Wealth II: Finance and Business Essentials for Medical Practices

Play to Prosper: The Passive Investor's Game Plan

Play to Prosper: The Small Investor's Survival Guide

Is a PhD for Me? Life in the Ivory Tower:
A Cautionary Guide for Aspiring Doctoral Students

Leveraging People for a Corporate Turnaround: Leadership and Management
Guide for Organizational Change (also available in Chinese)

The author may be reached at: yuval@pillarsofwealth.com
or: www.PillarsOfWealth.com

Online Course

Comprehensive <u>Online</u> Financial Literacy
Education Designed for Doctors.

Over 50 Videos.

Average Length: 5 minutes.

All Major Financial Planning Areas Covered.

Spreadsheet templates, Examples, Articles, and Links.

Visit Us At:

www.PillarsOfWealth.com

CPSIA information can be obtained
at www.ICGtesting.com
Printed in the USA
LVOW08s1746261116
514565LV00001B/1/P